Get ready to plunge, fully \
motherhood. With hilarious \
'Thriving and Surviving Raising \
adventure of parenting a large brood. Anne Perrottet is an Australian dynamo: her book shows how it's possible to manifest an abiding love for every child while fostering their sporting spirit, embracing their losses and fighting in their corner. As a mother of ten, I know that no one teaches you how to do this stuff. The story of how Perrottet worked it out for herself is thrilling.

Andrea Picciotti-Bayer, \
Director of the Conscience Project and mother of ten.

It cannot be easy to compress the wisdom gleaned from raising 13 children into 100 pages, but somehow Anne Perrottet has done it. The book is packed with tales of the many adventures she and her husband John had raising their large family. It's an entertaining and profitable read!

Andrew V. Abela, Ph.D. \
Dean, Busch School of Business \
The Catholic University of America

A heartwarming account of the beauty -and messiness- of life with 13 children that will make you laugh and cry, and then do it all again. Reading this book made me feel like I was sitting at the kitchen table with a good friend and hearing about her day. This story of family and faith, through the triumphs and tribulations, is an inspiration and one you won't want to miss.

April Readlinger, \
Executive Director, CanaVox

This is a charming and readable book by a woman who has truly loved being the mother of a very large family - a "baker's dozen" of children. Perhaps my favorite sections are those about her experiences coaching and watching her children's sporting events; and about her inventive strategies for getting the dishes and other household jobs done. Anne Perrottet's deep faith, her sense of humor, and her warmth shine through. A very engaging read!

Evelyn Birge Vitz.
Ph.D., Yale; M.A., Professor Emerita of French Literature, NYU.
Author of numerous books including 'In the Presence of Power: Court and Performance in the Premodern Middle East, Performing the Medieval Narrative', and the cookbook 'A Continual Feast'.
Mother of six children, grandmother of 23.

Chesterton observed that the "supreme adventure is being born... [When]we step into the family we step into a fairy-tale." In her entertaining and edifying book, Anne Perrottet proves his point. The life of carpools and chores, of birth and loss, of joys and sorrows is the *real* adventure. Lurking within every seemingly boring home is excitement, romance, and heartbreak. In the midst of it all is the encounter with God and the opportunity to grow in grace. Those with families of their own will understand and enjoy the book's stories and lessons. Those looking forward to the adventure of marriage and family will receive a better introduction than any catechism can provide!

Very Rev. Paul D. Scalia
Episcopal Vicar for Clergy
Diocese of Arlington
Pastor
Saint James Catholic Church

Anne Perrottet's account of her adventures as mother of a large and active family is simply delightful. Her stories show how the power of faith, hope, and love in family life give zest to every day—and happy memories for a lifetime.

James B. Stenson
Educator and author
Boston, USA

Wisdom comes in many forms, including the engaging stories of life and love told by a mother of thirteen! This delightful book offers lessons for achieving holiness and happiness, all while busy with the pruning and watering needed for the flowering of family and marriage.

Joseph Koterski, S.J.
Associate Professor of Philosophy,
Fordham University
Bronx NY

Full of warmth and wisdom, in "Thriving and Surviving Raising Thirteen", Anne Perrottet takes us on a very personal journey through motherhood, it's joys and heartbreaks, its many stretching moments, its sometimes near despair, and ultimately its rewards - not as an expert, but as a woman - who like many, are simply trying to do their best and, sometimes, but not always succeeding, yet never wavering in their determination to give their all for their children.

Maggie Hamilton
Australian writer and social researcher, who delights in new possibilities and dreams of an even better future for us all.

It is a rollicking great story…of life lived with the intensity of one who loves her children fiercely and loves their freedom even more. Within are loads of experiences to enjoy and ponder as you figure out a bit more how to shape your kids so they will have a blast shaping the world.

Pat Fagan
Former Executive Director of the Free Congress Foundation.
Former Secretary for Family and Social Policy at HHS under President George Herbert Bush.
Senior Fellow on Family Culture at the Heritage Foundation.
Founder and Former Director of Marriage and Religion Research institute at Family Research Council.
Director of Marriage and Religion Research Institute (MARRI).
Publisher and editor of Marripedia.org.

This book resonates with me greatly - there are so many laughs and so many good moments! I have a large family and Anne Perrottet tells it just like it is. Many more things are learned in the home than at school. A big family is a factory of future leaders. Raising children is a science, just like education. This is why I can highly recommend 'Thriving and Surviving Raising 13' which will be a great success!

Rosa Pich
Spanish author of "Rosa, What's Your Secret?", Speaker and
Mother of 18 children

Family life is essential to happiness. And in this beautiful book Anne Perrottet shares with readers the joys and sorrows of living family life well.

Ryan T. Anderson, Ph.D.,
President of the Ethics and Public Policy Center,
Witherspoon Institute of Princeton, New Jersey.

Thriving

and

Surviving
Raising Thirteen

Anne Perrottet

Connor Court Publishing

Published in 2022 by Connor Court Publishing Pty Ltd

Copyright © Anne Perrottet

Connor Court Publishing Pty Ltd

PO Box 7257

Redland Bay QLD 4165

sales@connorcourt.com

www.connorcourtpublishing.com.au

Phone 0497 900 685

ISBN: 9781922815057

Front Cover Illustration: Jen Charlton

Illustrations: Jen Charlton

Printed in Australia

Contents

Dedication

This book is lovingly dedicated to my husband, John – my best friend. Without whose love, generosity, and encouragement I could never have written this book or had anyone to write about for that matter!

To Madeleine, Alexander, Dominic, Charles, Joseph, Julien, Sophia, Oliver, Gabriel, Francesca, Veronique, Jean-Claude and Natasha – my amazing and talented children who have been my inspiration for so many of these incredible, moving and crazy stories.

I am truly honoured and blessed to be their Mother.

Acknowledgements

I would like to thank my wonderful husband, John who has always encouraged me to push myself and achieve what I sometimes thought impossible. He has been by my side supporting me at every turn. His unsurpassed patience, generosity, wisdom, calmness, and guidance has helped me overcome my own doubts instilling in me the determination to succeed. Thank you.

My eldest son, Alexander has been the driving force in bringing this book to completion. He has been my legal advisor, my editor, and my literary agent. His dedication, patience, encouragement, hard work, and sense of humour have been impressive and humbling. Thank you.

I am indebted to the persistence and encouragement of numerous friends and acquaintances who have asked me for years to write a book about raising my family. Thank you for not giving up on me and believing that one day I would deliver. I guess you all knew I had a lot of practice delivering!

Most importantly I would like to thank all my children who have been the inspiration for this book and my children-in-law and grandchildren who I am sure will be my inspiration for the next one. Stand by!

1

A Doll's House

When I was a kid I used to daydream, wishing my life was different.

My primary school held an annual raffle and one year the big prize was a doll's house. It was a beautiful house with a red roof with many rooms decorated with miniature wooden furniture. It had tables and chairs, lounges, a cute little kitchen and a bedroom with a canopy bed. That was going to be my bed if I won! It was displayed on a large table in the school playground under a huge oak tree where we used to eat lunch and where bats hung from its branches at night. I remember standing next to the table for what seemed like hours, looking down into the doll's house, imagining it to be mine.

I thought that I just had to win because if I did, my life would change. I would be happy and the people living in the house with me would be happy too.

But I didn't win that doll's house and my heart was broken.

I often thought about that little doll's house and whether it changed the life of the little girl who won it.

In time my broken heart mended and I began to dream again. I watched other people smiling and wondered what made them so happy. They couldn't all have a doll's house. There had to be something more. Maybe even something better.

In kindergarten I met Helen, my first 'best friend'.

She had 13 other brothers and sisters.

13!

And she was just about always happy. She used to say that if she ever felt she didn't have friends at school, then she had plenty waiting for her at home. I wanted that. Not just for myself, but I wanted my future kids to have that. That's how they would be happy – little figurines running around through the rooms of the doll's house, hiding under the canopy bed and helping out in the cute little kitchen; sleeping soundly in the little wooden beds without a fear or worry in the world.

But it would be real.

My parents divorced while I was at school. I was sent to boarding school for a short time while they tried to sort out their problems. I loved boarding school. It was small, meals were prepared which meant I didn't have to cook and the older students were happy to help with any study issues I had. My grades began to improve along with my self-esteem because I had some peace and quiet and direction to focus on my work and feel good about myself. I also became very close to some of my fellow boarders, as living together forged a special bond that the day pupils didn't have.

I was starving for a sense of belonging, but also the warmth and security that I suppose only a father can give. When I was at home in the breaks, I remember hiding behind the door in the laundry crying as I hugged Jan, our golden Labrador, aching to be understood and have a normal family life. I begged my mother to allow me to go back to boarding school but she needed my help at home. And so, once again distracted with my parents' problems, my marks began to drop, and along with them, my self-esteem, my hopes, and my big dreams.

When I left school I didn't know what to do. One day a friend asked me to go to Canberra and help out with a youth club. I had nothing better to do so I went. Who would have thought that Australia's capital city, with its bland paddocks, old, cold buildings and bitter cold temperatures would be my Damascus?

The people running that club were genuinely interested in me and how I was living my life. I thought I was going along to help, but bit by bit, I was the one growing. Someone was watering and feeding my soul. Eventually, I found a direction and enrolled in university to study education. The door to that doll's house was beginning to unlock and my life was beginning to change.

A few years later I met John at a party. He shared my Catholic faith; he was a good friend; he had a good sense of humour; and was rather good looking, which always helps.

And he wanted a large family.

Eventually he proposed… we got married and we built our own little doll's house.

One of my sons sent me a photo of it the other day – he drove by as we do every decade or so to indulge the memories and see if much has changed. It still has the jacaranda tree out the front that the kids used to climb, a generous hedge sheltering the house from the road, John's carport he built in the front drive and, around the back, the bushy backyard. It had a great Aussie BBQ, and terraced levels separated by retainer walls of concrete test cylinders. We would spend weekends going to Readymix, where he used to work, fill our old station wagon with them and bring them home to build what our neighbours called our 'Great Wall of China'.

As expected we soon ran out of room and extended the house, and John painstakingly laid hundreds of brick pavers out the back for the kids to play on and ride their little bikes without getting muddy every time. We added a kitchen, family room and laundry. It was a pale blue laminated kitchen with a sliding door into an un-tiled laundry. There would be no silent aching crying behind that door, I was determined of it.

There were no canopy beds, but the beds were starting to fill, with very cute little humans…

Ten years later that house really and truly felt like a doll's house. We had outgrown it and it was time to move on. Our new home not far away had two storeys, a swimming pool and reverse-cycle air conditioning upstairs. And children. Happy children – for the most part. Running around, hiding behind the lounges, making a mess in the kitchen and sleeping in their little wooden beds.

And as I sanitised stained nappies I realised my old dreams were sanitised too. But somehow I had what I wanted, and there in what used to be a void not far below the surface – I felt very happy. And they were happy too.

John worked for the World Bank. His work would often take him out of the country and I would power on at home with the young kids and explain that daddy would be home soon. I was energetic and put my teaching skills to work by getting them started early on words and numbers. Once when John was away, in a quiet moment while the children were taking their afternoon nap, I discovered I was pregnant.

Again.

I always loved finding out I was expecting another baby, but this time was different.

For some reason I felt a heavy cloud hanging over me, causing me to doubt myself and my ability to cope. Suddenly I worried, thinking John would be stressed about this impending newcomer and the extra financial burden it would place on our already struggling bank account. I was alone, and vulnerable.

The morning John was due to arrive home the kids were so excited. We prepared the house, and I dressed them up in their best outfits to welcome daddy home, all the while struggling to assemble a series of scrambled thoughts that were rushing through my mind.

I loaded the children into our white Toyota Tarago, with its navy and maroon stripes down the sides. It wouldn't be long before we replaced it with another life-long friend – a 15-seater manual Nissan Urvan. Those were the days before power steering, and driving that vehicle was a serious workout. It has now well and truly moved on, but I have an unbreakable bond with that van, and feel I might meet it in the afterlife… perhaps in purgatory!

All on board and buckled up, I drove to the airport and the kids clambered out of the Tarago and stood in line as I checked all looked presentable. After tucking in boys' shirts, straightening girls' dresses and patting down wisps of hair we marched into the airport and checked the arrivals screen. The kids loved going to the airport and why not? It was their second home! They loved all the frenzied activity of grandparents, parents and kids as well as all the pulling and pushing of colourful luggage and PA announcements.

But most importantly they were always so excited to see their daddy, emerging with a big smile and sometimes with some thoughtful gifts.

After all the hugs and kisses were over, we loaded the kids back into the Tarago and headed off to the beach to wait for the two oldest children to finish an English holiday program. It was a beautiful Spring morning at Pittwater, with the sun kissing the water and spreading its rays across the horizon, stretching from shore to shore. John and I sat on a low sandstone wall under palm trees holding hands as we watched the children swinging back and forth in the playground a few meters away. The breeze cooled my face and eased my nerves, but I was focused on picking the right moment to share my news.

Trying to delay the inevitable I asked how his trip went knowing he would explain in meticulous detail every frustrating conversation with colleagues and clients and every deal that did or didn't work. As he spoke my thoughts drifted back to those scrambled words still struggling to get organised in my head. I gave monosyllabic responses to the snippets of information I was retaining. When he drew breath I grabbed the opportunity to blurt out, "I need to tell you something."

Tears began to roll down my cheeks as I dropped my head and turned toward him. I didn't need to say a word. He held me tight and told me that he had a feeling I was pregnant. He was smiling and warm and lifted me up.

"How will we cope?" I cried.

I'll never forget his response.

"We have always coped in the past and we will cope in the future. I love you."

2

Birthing Stories

John and I have been through a lot together. And just as I was pruned and watered back in those days of growth in my late teens, I realised we needed to keep pruning and watering ourselves – and our marriage.

And sometimes that was hard.

Even though you know you may be pruning roses, it's always a shock and surprise to be pricked by a thorn.

Our first and last children were the only ones who arrived on time. Most of the others sluggishly emerged two weeks later. On the morning of 20 May 1980, John left for work and I promptly went into labour.

I had some idea, from movies of course, of what to expect. We started romantically, with John meeting me with flowers, then brunch at a café, as we nonchalantly called the hospital to let them know we, and one other, were about to arrive.

An hour later I was prepped and organised for delivery with John sitting patiently by my bedside reading the newspaper waiting for the intravenous drip to take effect and to see some action. He soon tired of reading the paper and looked for a pen and notebook to document everything that was happening to me. He started writing... 'Anne is experiencing slight discomfort, intravenous drip inserted, nurses are monitoring the baby's heart rate, Anne's blood pressure taken, pain increasing, contractions are 10 minutes apart,' and so on. He was just as excited as I was and that was his way of giving birth with me, I suppose. But when the contractions became more intense and I needed his support, he put down his notes for later.

He rubbed my back, pressed on my hips as I lay on my side which seemed to ease the pain; gave me ice to suck on; and kept suggesting people we could think of that needed prayers and offerings – it was a special way to see through a painful moment and I really believed that somehow I was helping those good friends of ours that were also going through some pain in their lives.

But what really kept me going was the thought that very soon I would be cuddling my first child.

The baby was born, and John, exhausted, went home to recover.

And during his convalescence he transcribed and embellished his notes into a little notebook, just a common one from the newsagent, with a royal red cover, with black tipped corners. We called it the *Red and Black Book*, and we vowed to keep writing in it – the ups and downs, joys and sorrows and funny moments of this baby's life. We'd include our words of love and affection, perhaps some words of complaint and frustration, but we'd leave out the sorrows.

As our family grew so did the *Red and Black Books*. We kept making sure to buy the same style book. They never seemed to run out of stock, and we never seemed to run out of stories.

Today they are like historical manuscripts, brought out at birthdays with the juicy bookmarked stories read out. An evening birthday celebration starts with a favourite meal, cake and lollies, and then we settle in to a session with the books – I start reading and John takes over when I start crying. Most of the books begin from the time I was pregnant, others from their first moments on earth and one, the moment he entered Heaven.

We have documented all their 'firsts': achievements at school, friends, parties, tantrums, getting in trouble at school, and embarrassing moments that make them blush when we read them out years later. Stories that make us all laugh even though we have read them again, and again, year after year.

When the first one grew up and got married, we decided it was time. I put down my pen, closed the *Red and Black Book* in the silence of our bedroom, and thanked God for this child and how she found happiness with her husband. I found some big ribbon, wrapped up her books with a big bow and presented them to her after John gave his wedding speech.

This has become a family tradition when our children marry. And now that I'm finally running out of books, I've written this one.

3

Diving in Deep

In theology classes I learned God doesn't just give us a soul at the start of our lives, but his act of creation is continuous – he keeps us in existence all our lives.

That's intense.

And it's just what parenting felt like. As if the pain of childbirth wasn't enough, I felt I had to be constantly on watch to prevent my children doing harm to themselves. One fell off my bed a couple of times, some kept getting lost at the shops, and others seemed to have a fascination with the bottom of the swimming pool.

After all, they don't teach parenting at university. You just find yourself one day in the deep end, under water. Fully clothed.

We were blessed to have a wonderful kidney bean-shaped pool in our backyard, which was a godsend in the hot Australian summers. The kids would sometimes come out for dinner and dive back in later, swimming and playing games well into the dark evening, with the pool lights on. It seemed to have godly powers – it could sustain life, and in a second, it could almost take it away. On a typically hot day, one son with a keen desire to keep up with his big brothers was diving and flipping into the pool, with his float strapped to his back. Sitting on the elevated verandah with my lime ice block I may have looked like a relaxed sunbather, but no, on the other side of my sunglasses my eagle eyes were scanning back forth, keeping watch.

I kept waiting for him to re-surface but after a few seconds I realised his float was actually preventing him from making a complete turn, trapping him, with his face under the water. The other kids hadn't realised and were having too much fun to hear my screams. I charged down the stairs, across the lawn, threw open the pool gate, and dived in the pool, fully clothed, in the deep end, and pulled him out.

Despite other further attempts, this son is still alive today, constantly safeguarding his own children.

But I can't pretend to have always been the hero.

One had a nappy drenched in red urine as I didn't read the label before feeding her an undiluted bottle of concentrated berry drink. Another one was raced to the hospital after he knocked back two half-filled glasses of wine we had left on the kitchen window ledge. He was about four years old – old enough to climb up and steal the wine, but too young to understand why a doctor was shoving tubes into his nostrils and pumping out the wine. He thought we were trying to kill him. We often joked later that it had a permanent effect on him as he was rather quirky and daring, but at the time I felt all the emotions of guilt, fear and at times helplessness. Why wasn't I there? Why didn't anyone warn me about this? Will these kids make it to adulthood? When does the self-preservation instinct actually kick in?

One morning, at a time when those negative emotions were long in the past and I exuded confidence and control – the way I liked to rule my house – I got the kids dressed and loaded them into the van for some errands. I had laid a two-week-old bundle of joy on the bed, left to contemplate the ceiling as babies so often must do, as I washed and dressed and buckled up the others in the van.

I thought I was so clever and well organised especially with a new little one in tow! I reversed out of the driveway past the homemade wooden basketball posts, let the back tyres kiss the kerb on the other side of the street, and then pushed the gear stick into position as the Urvan groaned up the street. Neighbours familiar with the sound of the car, and the noise of the kids, turned to wave and smile – always a good sign that our most recent misdemeanour had been forgotten, or at least forgiven.

Driving out one of the side streets and into the main road I looked through the rear-view mirror scanning the rows of grey vinyl seats making sure all the children were present and accounted for. Checking all were buckled up and settled, my eyes came to rest on the baby capsule locked in the seat behind me. Suddenly my foot hit the brake as I screamed, "Shit, I forgot the baby!"

I panicked.

I had to get off the road but it was going to be rather difficult with massive trucks thundering down behind me, and cars switching sharply from lane to lane. Eventually, I maneuvered the van to the outside lane and turned left into the closest side street and sped home. Zooming down the street and into the driveway I jumped out of the van, skipped up the front stairs two by two, barged through the front door and into my bedroom where the sleeping beauty lay completely oblivious to the last 15 minutes of stress.

Young children think their parents can do anything and everything – I didn't blame them, as they saw me running up flights of stairs, jumping fully clothed into the pool and maneuvering that Urvan. But soon, one of my daughters was talking me into coaching a basketball team. With seven sons, I knew more about rugby than basketball and I had to confess that I didn't even know all the rules. Feeling a twinge of guilt for spending too much time talking to the mums on the sideline I agreed, hesitantly, to coach the Under 8's & 9's little basketballers.

But I am not a half-measures person. I dive in, fully clothed – in the deep end.

We trained every Tuesday afternoon rain, hail or shine. Training was exhausting. I pushed them as well as myself for an hour of strength-building exercises; laps around the oval; and shooting skills. I had some catching up to do with the rulebook, but I kept one step ahead of them, teaching new moves I had read about the night before!

And to top it all off and warm down, we finished with something different – yoga relaxation exercises, which the girls now well into their twenties still talk about. I found coaching somewhat like parenting. I strived to be fair and unbiased yet demanding – so each girl could reach her potential. I promised equal court-time regardless of talent, as long as they came to training, and unless we were vying for the semi-final or grand final.

During one game I subbed one girl off. She happened to be the best player on the team, but only slightly better than my two daughters – so the coach thought! Oblivious to everything around me except the game I yelled, "Dribble, pass, don't travel, focus, get aggressive, shoot, watch for rebounds keep close to your partner, and remember what you learned at training!"

After a while one of the mums tapped me on the shoulder and pointed to the little girl, sitting on the bench in tears. I sat on the bench next to her and asked what the matter was.

The matter was that she knew she was the best player.

And despite my efforts to use reason, the tear factory was in full production. I told her "I don't think Michael Jordan cried when he was subbed off" but that didn't work. The only thing we were shedding more than tears at this stage were points…

We needed this crying basketballer back on court. But she needed to learn to be a team player and accept her time on the bench just like her team mates.

So I struck a deal – if she stopped crying I'd call 'time out' and she could go back on. Those crocodile tears quickly disappeared, and she was back shooting those baskets in no time. After the game I had a chat with her dad who was a great basketballer himself. He thanked me and told me he didn't know how to be firm with his little girl. He was a wonderful man with such a big soft heart but needed to show some tough love. Sadly, a few years later that young dad passed away. I never had a problem with his little girl again as we moved up the ladder, winning the semi-final and then the grand final!

John has also been a cricket coach, an athletics coach, a public speaking and debating mentor, and a loud voice on the sidelines of rugby games, so much so that people today imitate his trademark call: "C'moooooooon Redfield!!!" I used to stand on the sidelines of my sons' soccer games and threaten no dinner if they didn't kick the ball. We prepared half-time oranges, washed jerseys and strategised from the sidelines. One Saturday we drove home hurriedly before the game could begin – all the jerseys had been sent home with my son for cleaning, and he had left the smelly things in the back of his cupboard.

Some of the most satisfying moments have been watching my children dive into something, and I learnt from that day by the pool that you have to be ready to dive in with them, fully clothed, in the deep end.

4

Triumph and Disaster

I was never a rugby coach and perhaps my boys are lucky for that, or they may not have finished a game. Once when John was away, I drove my two young teenage boys to their rugby game, mouthguards – check; boots – check; headgear – check. Parents were milling along the sideline rugged up in coats, beanies and gloves trying to thaw out in the impotent winter's sun. But the voices fell silent when loud rap music and the deep hum of supercharged cars pierced the atmosphere, and the convoy came to a stop near our field.

Grown men emerged. Large ones. I don't know which Polynesian country their heritage was but they looked like they could be fathers to some of our boys. Hairy legs like tree trunks, face stubble, and hey – hadn't they driven the cars to the game? Two of my boy's particularly slim legs would have been the width of one of their arms! While our rugby players had a reputation for punching above their weight and defeating much bigger opposition, this game was bordering on the ridiculous.

I felt sick with foreboding.

When these man-boys ran out onto the field I could feel the ground shake. It sent shivers up my spine. They reminded me of 'Bluto the Terrible' from the Popeye animated cartoon series. It was 15 Blutos versus 15 Popeyes whose mothers hadn't fed them their can of spinach that morning!

It was going to be a massacre...

We were genuinely concerned for the safety of our sons. The giants had the ball for the majority of the game. Our boys were being knocked down like flies and some were not getting back up. It looked more like a battlefield than a rugby field.

Before long play stopped and not because of a try. Some boy was down, injured on the other side of the field and I couldn't see who. Every mother prayed it was someone else's son. I asked the boy who had been cheering next to me if he could run over and check who it was.

He came back and delivered me the news like I was a war widow.

I'd had enough.

I marched onto the field. He wasn't moving. I felt sick. Thankfully, the father of one of our players was a doctor and had a look at him. His prognosis was there were no broken bones but a possible concussion and advised us to take him to the hospital for a thorough examination.

I was so fired up that I yelled at the referee for even allowing such a game to start in the first place. I also demanded the coach call off the game immediately. I told him we came to watch a rugby game not a blood sport!

Well, the game wasn't going to be called off, so I took my remaining fully-conscious son off the field as well. He was not happy, but I didn't care. In the emergency ward the inevitable conversations took place. I sang the virtues of tennis, or golf, of facing your fears – yes – but within reason. My sons did not take it well. There was no way to separate them from this love of their lives. Still, I persisted with my suggestions to take up golf. Incredibly, one week later, a young high school girl from the local community was struck on the back of her head by a golf ball and tragically passed away.

My argument evaporated.

By the time the grand final came along, they were in the thick of it again and I was resigned to watch and pray from the sideline. The scene was set as usual – the scrawny under 10s were up against the beasts from the West. They were dressed in black like the All Blacks and looked just as formidable.

The atmosphere in the family that week was electrifying. It was hard to tell who wanted to win more, our son playing in the team, or the two older brothers who were the coaches. One of them had even attended the opposition's semi-final games to gain valuable intelligence on their style of play. The boys were given their pre-game pep talk while the bleachers were flooded with fans wearing the red and blue team colours. The boys were so nervous in the shed before the game that when asked if anyone needed to go to the toilet before kick off, they all rushed to the cubicles. We were excited too, but felt sick in anticipation of what lay ahead. Wests ran onto the field with roars from the crowd. The roars were even louder when our lean and wiry boys ran through a tunnel of coaches, families, teachers, and students. As they faced their opposition in the middle of the field to shake hands before the game, it really did look like a bunch of school kids meeting the All Blacks. A complete mismatch.

The boys kicked off and then tackled like their lives depended on it. The atmosphere on the sidelines was tense. Parents, teachers, and students yelled and screamed "Run, tackle, step, p-a-s-s the ball!!!!!" John repeatedly hollered out his notorious war cry, "C'moooooooon Redfield", "Gooooooo you Redfield!" The game was close and the coaches were visibly under stress. They paced up and down the sidelines with furrowed brows as they scrutinised the game and fired instructions from opposite sides of the field. Their mobile phones relayed coaching tips from passionate and jittery dads as our boys tried their best to gain ground. At one point a Redfield boy kicked the ball the entire way down the field, with his teammates sprinting after it in chase, only for the biggest player from Wests to pick it up preventing a try. By half-time the score was even, one try each.

The tension was mounting but so was our confidence as the game moved into the nail-biting second half. Whenever we had the ball our boys kept to the game plan of kicking the ball down the other end of the field to wear out their opponents. When they had the ball our boys defended, tackled and wrestled. Oftentimes a whole child was dragged down the field like an annoying pest clinging obdurately to the bootstraps of the large but somewhat uncoordinated opposition. I was stunned at their bravery and wondered how their tenaciousness and determined spirit could be bottled and used for other purposes like study and jobs at home!

Eventually, some clever field position and superior speed resulted in a try to give us the lead. But how could the stringy Redfield boys defend their lead against such a formidable opposition?

The supporters were starting to tire from the intensity and the shouting. We were at a local rugby field but it felt like we were in an Olympic stadium. I felt goosebumps on my arms, wondering if our little midgets with huge hearts could hold on to their miracle lead. Camped on their own try-line for what seemed like hours, they formed a human wall and tackled, and tackled and tackled. At one stage the referee blew his whistle to pull apart a ruck, and as bodies unfurled from the pile, my weedy son staggered out like a crumpled piece of paper, desperate for the final whistle to sound.

The whistle blew. The game was over. They had won!!! The opposition coach said he had never seen anything like it. I have often thought back to that game and marveled at how humans can become so inspired and motivated about some things, and not about others.

We all have our interests and inspirations.

I was a swimmer, John, a runner. He represented his school at some of those posh Sydney North Shore athletics carnivals and it was clear early on that our children had inherited the lean stature and the running gene. I attended probably a hundred cross-country races. They are more interesting than the ones around the oval, as they go off and disappear for a while and then later come back into view and you have to wait and see how close to the front your child is, like waiting for your bag to come out at the airport carousel.

One year I decided not to go – it was my son's final year at school and he had been too pre-occupied with study to make a serious commitment to cross-country training. This was going to be a 'fun run' for him so apparently it wasn't worth me attending.

Later that morning I received a phone call from his school. The secretary told me they had called an ambulance but she wouldn't say why. I piled the pre-school kids in the van and it groaned all the way up the road to the school. I wanted to hold down the horn all the way telling people to get out of my way as my son was dying! I had no idea whether he was alive or dead. Thankfully one of my older sons was at home at the time and drove to the school with me. We passed through the main gates and parked outside the school office. He rushed in and was told his brother was down the back of the school near the dam.

I didn't hesitate to test the Urvan's off-road capabilities, and drove right across one of the playing fields, to where my son lay under a giant willow tree near the dam. Pulling up the brake I allowed myself to think, for a split-second, that it looked like a nice enough place to die, if you must. But then I jumped out of the car and ran toward him. I knelt next to him. He was packed with ice under each arm, between his legs, and behind his head. Kneeling beside him I held his hand in mine and kissed his forehead. He asked me if he was in danger of death. I told him I didn't know and to say an act of contrition while I asked someone to find a priest. I told the ambulance man that we usually go to a particular hospital. He snapped back and told me my son will go to where he will get the best treatment. I began to worry. He was in deep trouble.

All this while I had no idea how it happened, or what was wrong.

Eventually I was told that my son had made a split-second decision before the race to go hard. It was his last year at school, and he believed he could win it. With no training.

At one stage in the race he made a break from the leading pack and kept up a blistering pace, the taste of victory overcoming his pain and his very real dehydration. Coming around the side of the oval in 40-degree heat, sweating like a pig with his parched tongue dying for water and only 500 metres to go, that sweet taste of victory suddenly turned sour.

He started to wobble and to see double. His pace dropped right off and he tottered around before collapsing on the ground. His first friends on the scene say he started ripping blades of grass out of the ground, crawling around in a stupor and hallucinating saying he was possessed and needed a priest to exorcise him!

Teachers and students ran to help. One of his good friends realised how serious it was and ordered students – and even teachers – to send for help. He went to get ice from the staff room and was refused, until he forced his way in, yelling that my son was dying and ordering them to call an ambulance! Not long afterwards the first responders arrived and with great effort, stabilised him. They took him straight to hospital and he remained there on a drip, for days.

My kids have collected plenty of trophies and medals over the years and like to compare and compete. But I always boast of my trophies in the glass cabinet – their small Christening Cups engraved with their baptismal dates. I don't want to lose them, nor the kids they represent! And I would tell them that until they grow up and have their own kids, no matter how many gold-looking plastic trophies they collect, their real trophies are their good friends.

A few days later I had to go back to the school to collect some study books as my son had to take two weeks off school. Standing in the classroom doorway I saw the student who gave up his medal to save my son's life. I walked in, straight past the maths teacher and turned every head in the room. I gave him a big hug and thanked him for saving my son's life.

5

Joseph's Lesson

By the time we had four babies we had learnt a lot. I had learnt not to leave glasses of red wine on a window ledge for starters. And we both learnt about febrile convulsions, swimming pools, funnel web spiders and other things that could all too quickly take the life of my little treasures if I wasn't careful.

And before we were ready for another child, and more lessons to learn, we had a real surprise.

Once again I found myself in the ultrasound chair, the radiologist rubbing cold gel on my tummy and pushing and prodding here and there, taking measurements, pressing the keys on the keyboard, clicking and dragging the mouse. When she had finished I asked for the photo but she hesitated, and said she'd send it to my doctor.

I thought that was rather unusual.

I left without the photo and headed home to pick up the kids from my in-laws. Once home, they were playing on their bikes, charging across the yard, over the rows of brick pavers John had laid. Such energy. I brought out their lunch and the four of them sat at their little yellow plastic table and chairs chatting and laughing. Soon it was bath-time and the evening routine began.

They splashed about in the old cast-iron pink bath making so much noise that I didn't hear the phone ring. My eldest child took the call and told me a friend of mine wanted to speak to me. I left her in charge of the kids while I went to the phone.

It was my obstetrician. He delivered my first four babies and had never called me at home before.

What he said next will never leave me.

"Your baby has an abnormality preventing any possibility of living".

I was stunned.

"What do you mean, what sort of abnormality?"

Anencephaly, as I was to find out, means the baby doesn't have a brain, or complete skull, which makes it very hard to live after birth.

My knees weakened beneath me as I dropped onto the chair next to the phone. I didn't know what to do. For a moment, I forgot he was still on the line as I held a tea towel to my mouth. I was so shocked I couldn't speak, or even cry. And if I was numbed by what he had just said, then I was shocked by the next thing.

"You could have an abortion."

I felt sick and violated by those words. I hugged my tummy wanting to protect my unborn baby from any further harm. The doctor may well have just asked me if I wanted to kill one of my other children.

"I thought you knew my opinion on abortion?"

He did suggest I ask for a second and more accurate opinion from a specialist.

I stayed in the chair in total disbelief. I knew I should ring John but I couldn't speak. Soon the kids came looking for me and asked why I was so upset.

I told them our baby was going to die. I shouldn't have said that but it just came out.

Finally, I gathered the strength to ring John. I told him our baby was very sick. He asked how sick? I replied he was going to die. There was silence on the other end of the phone. "What?" He asked. I told him, just like the doctor did, that our baby didn't have a brain.

He left work immediately and came home.

I finished bathing the children and preparing dinner. I needed to keep busy. I needed to do something. When John arrived home we just hugged. I couldn't express how I felt. I couldn't speak. I walked through the laundry and out the side of the house to the backyard. John followed. I know he felt helpless and lost for words but I couldn't help him. I took the clothes off the line and folded them into the basket. I wish I could have burst into tears and sob all my feelings out but I just couldn't. I was numb. I didn't know how to feel or what to say. I think John felt the same.

We made an appointment with the specialist the next morning and organised the children to stay with friends. After a cup of tea we headed off to the hospital. I dissolved into tears a couple of times as we drove along praying the Rosary. We were praying for a miracle and the grace to cope with whatever lay ahead.

It was a cold and rainy day as we arrived at Royal North Shore Hospital in North Sydney for the second opinion. The doctor confirmed the worst, prompting a series of questions. "Was it something I did?" "Was it my diet?" "Did I do too much exercise?"

"No, no and no. It is genetic and it is no one's fault."

I felt slightly relieved. He went on to explain that John and I would go through the grieving process: denial, anger, bargaining, depression and acceptance.

We walked away together in silence and decided to go to that little café where we romantically met before the birth of our first baby. Back when we were bright-eyed and naïve and didn't have a worry in the world. This time was so different. We sat opposite each other lost in thought when I said to John, "You know this grieving process the doctor talked about? I think we went through all that over the weekend". We were shocked and couldn't believe it – denial. I don't think we were angry, there's no one to blame. Bargaining? May be if you call bargaining asking God to make things different. Depression? I don't think so, but sadness – yes. Acceptance? I feel I have accepted it. I don't like the idea but God has allowed it for some reason beyond our understanding.

I didn't feel like eating but knew I needed something to give me some energy. We settled on the soup. I needed to know more about our baby and asked John to take me to the local library. I needed to know what our baby would look like. In the back of my mind I recall the doctor telling us that the deformity would be significant. We found a book. The photos were shocking. Even my wild imagination hadn't thought up something like that. John suggested we go as we were just making it tougher on ourselves.

This was something that happened to other people, not to us. My husband and I felt numb for a long time. I was 16 weeks pregnant. We were told our baby could be born at any time, so we started studying the condition a little more to prepare for what lay ahead.

The helplessness led me to turn to God more, and I started asking Him to work a miracle and let our baby live. And if that was not to be, then I would completely spoil him and shower him with gifts in the short time we had together. I wanted to make up for all the birthday parties I would not be able to give him, all the hugs and kisses he was not going to receive and all the Christmases and other family times we were not going to share.

I don't know which stages of grief we went through, but there were difficult times. John and I were almost on different roller coasters of feelings. We had so many questions that couldn't be answered and at times felt distant from one another, lost in our own thoughts and emotions. I wondered how he felt towards me now that I was carrying such a deformed little baby. I felt embarrassed and tempted to think he might reject me. When I told him that, he told me he felt even closer than ever and wanted to protect me more. Somehow through it all we were more united and stronger and I suppose it was our special little baby that was bringing us closer in many ways.

Like every other child we had, we deliberately hadn't found out the sex. Every other time we'd be preparing clothes and bassinets and other items, but we knew that would be pointless. So what could we do to prepare for this baby, who was preparing for a very different life – the afterlife? If that really was where this child was headed, so swiftly, we wanted to know more about it.

If he or she was going to be in Mary's arms rather than mine, what would that be like? How would She look after our child? Would She kiss and hug our baby like we would? I thought about this often. My heart ached.

I wanted to have a funeral, even though people were saying we didn't need to. We spoke to our parish priest asking for a Mass, flowers, some music and a little white coffin and a white car. This baby was going to get the whole enchilada, as I couldn't give him anything else in this life.

The priest said we could have anything we wanted for our baby. He was a terrific priest.

But it was difficult to arrange. I was preparing to bury someone who had just started to grow and was very much alive. The way he kicked inside me – I couldn't believe he was going to die. My in-laws suggested we bury our baby in a plot where a couple of John's relatives were buried. We visited the cemetery to check it out. I will never forget parking our car and walking with a map in hand toward the grave. It was horrible. It was overgrown with weeds and partly caved in. No thanks.

That week I rang the cemetery. It is amazing just how much it costs to bury someone. A very compassionate man answered the phone. He asked on whose behalf was I arranging this. I explained it was for my unborn baby. There was a moment of silence. He told me there was a special area for little babies and asked me if I would like our baby to be buried there. I was so relieved as I wanted something new and beautiful for him. I explained we didn't have much money and he offered to give us this little plot of grass for costs. How kind he was.

The pregnancy progressed normally with our little baby kicking, pushing and enjoying his time with us. We didn't tell many people that he was going to die as I didn't want to be pitied. But it was hard to pretend that all was going well when we knew what lay ahead. I cherished every moment I had with him, but it was a powerless feeling not being able to help him. We could only watch and wait.

Three weeks out, I had contractions and all I could think about was the excitement of having a beautiful little baby. But our baby was not going to be beautiful.

Even though, as suddenly as they arrived, all my worries over those abnormalities vanished. In all the months we had prayed so much, we were far more interested in his soul, which was soon to make its journey to its proper home – the one we'll all have to make some day.

Our baby's birthday soon arrived, one week late, on 11 March 1985. It was a long labor and I could feel the baby's little legs kicking around inside me. It still gave me hope that he or she would be perfect and we would take our baby home. We were praying for a miracle right up to the end. The doctor baptised our baby in utero, "I baptise you Marie-Claire or Joseph John in the name of the Father, the Son and the Holy Spirit." That meant a lot to us, to receive that sacrament in such a special way.

Our baby boy was delivered feet first.

I looked toward John and when I saw his face, I knew our baby had died.

There was no hope left. There was no cry. Just silence. But not an empty silence – it was calm and grace-filled. His little heart stopped only a few moments before his birth. He was born into Heaven on 11 March 1985. We had been given a little saint, Joseph John.

I didn't get to hold him straight away. I looked across at him lying on a little table with his tiny chest not rising and falling. My arms ached to hold him and it seemed like ages before he was placed in my arms. To me he was beautiful.

When the nurse opened the bunny rug to show us his body, a thread of saliva reached from his mouth and clung to the little white blanket he was wrapped in. To this day whenever I think of Joseph I think of that thread of saliva, which was the only glimmer of life in his little body. The nurse was so sensitive to how we were feeling as she gently unwrapped our baby showing us his perfect arms and legs and little toes. He had the same cute nose and mouth as the other children.

The nurse lifted his lifeless hand and placed it in mine. I wanted that moment to last forever.

God's grace filled the room. It was not depressing at all. I will never forget the look on Joseph's little face. We could not wish him back. What he must have been experiencing was so glorious that it penetrated his little body. I am convinced he was experiencing the Beatific Vision. He was the lucky one, and we were honored to be his parents. This child had not been with us long, yet he taught us so many lessons about unselfish love; strength, sensitivity, fortitude, detachment and our purpose here on earth.

The funeral was so sad yet beautiful. When our parish priest, Fr Vaughan walked down the short aisle it felt like the beginning of the end. It was closure. But I wasn't ready to say goodbye. The congregation stood and to this day I can still feel my legs going to jelly. It was so hard. We buried him with all the other babies and little children in the 'Baby Lawn' section at Northern Suburbs Cemetery. Whenever we get a chance, we visit that cemetery. When I stand there looking at the plaque at the head of the grave, the memories come flooding back.

JOSEPH JOHN PERROTTET

BORN AND DIED 11th MARCH 1985

OUR LITTLE ONE

WHO TAUGHT US SO MUCH

WE SHALL TREASURE THE MOMENT

WE HAD TOGETHER FOREVER

I hadn't thought at the time that there was any more room in that burial plot, but 34 years later one of our sons and his wife had a similar situation. Their little one died just before she was born. It was heartbreaking yet very special to watch them carrying the little white coffin from the church with their precious daughter, Juliette close to their hearts. It was the same church John and I were married in and the same one they were married in. Tears flowed silently as they lowered their little girl into the ground where we said our goodbyes to Joseph so many years before.

Over the years Joseph has never been far away. We have prayed to him to keep a watchful eye on his brothers and sisters, and I have treated him just like any of the others, complaining when he doesn't do what I ask immediately. Slowly he has become more obedient over the years, just like his siblings.

We celebrate his birthday every year. And we read his very short but emotional Red and Black Book.

I used to make birthday cakes from that famous Woman's Weekly book that so many children of the 80's and 90's remember. It has ballerinas and trains, sports scenes and furry animals, of all shapes, colours and sizes, and all variety of lollies and sweets decorating them. Each year one child would get to choose Joseph's cake.

"Which one do you think we should make?" I asked one of my sons.

"This one," he said.

"The rocket! So it can shoot straight up to Joseph in Heaven."

6

Chaos and Crackpots

There were some things I had to do to prevent becoming a crackpot. I had to be tough, but not get too invested in my kids' problems to drive myself crazy. And I had to be clever to seek some moments of solace when I could, separating the girls from the boys and having some quiet time.

On an ordinary afternoon, I collected the girls from school first, before the boys. We chatted about how their day went and what homework they needed to do that afternoon. But before long the van rattled through the gates and lurched to a stop in front of the sandy-coloured pavement of the boys' school pick-up line. Thankfully, they were all present and accounted for so I didn't have to park the van and scour the five-acre property looking for them. With one hard yank on the door handle there was a breach in our defences and the marauding hordes charged in.

Throwing their backpacks into the van, six boys jostled and elbowed their way to be the first to lay claim to the best seat. I never understood why they preferred one seat over the others as there wasn't much difference between any of them really. It wasn't like we had business and economy class in the Urvan.

"Hi boys how'd your day go?" I asked, as they filed pass giving me a cursory kiss before settling down the back of the van while the girls wiggled up the front to find some refuge. We drove back up the drive and before reaching the gates their usual squabbling began. I turned left onto the road and we hadn't reached the first of four roundabouts before their voices reached such a crescendo it swamped us in unrelenting tsunami waves from the back of the van. I thought surely after a grueling day studying and playing sport they would be exhausted and too tired to fight. But oh no, not my sons!

I asked for silence, I pleaded for peace, I tried to distract them. And in the end I threatened to withdraw privileges. Nothing worked. My head was pounding, the girls were complaining and the traffic was stressful.

I couldn't take it anymore. And I didn't care if other people thought I was a crackpot.

I reached the roundabout and waited as cars zoomed in and out from every possible direction. I gripped the steering wheel so firmly my knuckles turned white as I pressed the accelerator and went in. But as I approached the middle of the roundabout I slammed my foot on the brake and came to a complete stop. Pressing on the horn I anchored my hand to it, simultaneously bringing all my boys to its attention, as well as everyone on the road, and possibly, the suburb.

I could tell the boys had stopped fighting. There was no other sound, but my horn, and well, perhaps the horns of quite a few other cars, as they began queuing up behind me. My 16-year-old daughter who had been in the passenger seat beside me had slunk to the floor in shame.

"How long would you like to stay in the middle of the roundabout?" I asked.

Shocked silence inside. More horns outside. And I couldn't care.

I slowly lifted my hand off the horn, moved into first gear and drove out of the roundabout, and out of everyone's way. It was a serious and perhaps risky investment, but it earned me a good ten to fifteen minutes of silence.

All the way home.

You can never be too creative in trying new ideas and new systems, to see if they work. We had various systems of cleaning up after dinner, with or without a dishwasher, in teams, in pairs, sometimes one person going it alone. That actually worked out best because as it turns out, it's hard to fight with yourself.

Of course, there was a roster of some kind, but if someone was repeatedly reprimanded during the meal there was always the threat… "Do you want the kitchen?"

For some reason one night there was a lot of talking and a great deal of commotion going on during dinner and it was difficult to gain some semblance of order. Our 15-year-old son kept answering back with uncharacteristic belligerence and was completely out of line. The tension grew around the table as he was pushing his luck more and more despite warnings of punishment. The non-offending children sat around the kitchen table grinning in silence, raising their eyebrows at each other and probably praying that he tested our patience a little more.

What bothered me most was his complete lack of respect in the way he muttered self-righteous responses under his breath. There was no remorse on his part so it was pointless to do anything else but pronounce the mandatory sentence: "You have the kitchen, for a week! Dinner is over!"

The other kids could hardly control their elation, smirking and giving each other invisible high fives. So, with a bad attitude and a sink full of suds he intentionally began clinking glasses, rattling cutlery and clanging pots as he began the first night of his sentence. Even while in solitary confinement in the kitchen he continued to rant and rave, so I converted his sentence to the maximum.

"OK you've got it for the whole term."

The others were in ecstasy. They couldn't believe I wasn't joking.

Over the ensuing couple of weeks he appealed the decision, saying the sentence was excessive for one night of madness. Judges must be just but also merciful, so he was granted parole, but on a strict good behaviour bond. Thereafter, whenever dinnertime laws are transgressed, the chant arises… "Kitchen! Kitchen! Kitchen!" As they thumped their fists on the table hoping John or I would hand down the sentence.

Punishment is so important, as it gives children a taste of real life. Endless threats are useless if children don't believe you're capable of following through. And there's no use getting worked up about it – you do the crime, you do the time. But they can't be straitjacketed and permanently corralled – they need to feel free to express themselves and be themselves without the constant fear of reprimand.

It came time for the weekly pilgrimage to the supermarket, with seven children under the age of twelve.

I parked the van near a trolley bay and unloaded the babies and toddlers into one trolley while my eldest daughter pushed the empty one behind me. Up and down the aisles we went throwing in groceries as the children implored, "Can we have this?" "Can we have that?"

'Yes", "No", "Maybe" "Let me think about it".

As I maneuvered my baby-laden trolley down through the vegetable bins the erratic and meandering trolley behind me was fast approaching. The driver was completely out of control eyeing off the goodies on either side of the aisle rather than paying attention to the traffic in front of her. The trolley finally came to a brutal stop – on my heels. I just about had enough. As I stopped to turn around and arrest the driver, the other prisoners seized the day and escaped from my trolley, running in all directions in what must have been for them a wondrous battlefield of laser tag.

What could I reasonably do? I just let go of any feeling of control.

But they were my kids. I couldn't just pretend I didn't know them.

Hobbling after them I pushed my childless trolley past a little old lady seeking refuge behind a corflute for crumpets and honey as she scolded, "What naughty children! I've never seen such behaviour in all my life!"

Suddenly my energies for discipline morphed into a feeling of protective loyalty.

"Well honey maybe you've forgotten what it was like to be a child or how your mother probably coped with your own behaviour!"

Moving through the aisles quickly loading up the trolley with the weekly supplies I could hear the children laughing and screaming somewhere in the store so I knew they were safe. Once I tracked them down, I gave them all a huge hug, their excitable faces bewildered with my inexplicable change of mood.

Passing through the checkout, there were no lollies or sweets that day due to the riot, but that old lady's lack of empathy somehow managed to save them from any worse fate.

One morning before school, I left the older children at home to get ready for school and have breakfast on their own as I went out for an early-morning meeting. I felt a little apprehensive but it was time they learned to be responsible and independent. When I returned home and pulled into the garage, I could see the schoolbags were no longer on the hooks on the wall, meaning they had left to catch the bus. I felt a sense of accomplishment and pride in their efforts.

I unbuckled the pre-schoolers and opened the door. The kids bounded up the stairs and into the kitchen. I followed holding the baby. I gasped as I lifted my feet over half-eaten crusts of toast and walked past smears of vegemite on the staircase wall. The kitchen table was covered with crumbs, spilt orange juice and overturned cups. The place was a mess. A disaster.

My blood pressure began to rise. I couldn't wait 24 hours to respond, I couldn't even count to ten before I lifted the phone.

I didn't call John.

I rang the school.

I asked the secretary to have my six sons waiting for me out the front of the school in 30 minutes. They were coming home to pay for their crime. The secretary contacted the boys' tutor who then called me back. I gave the poor man an ear full about how selfish and irresponsible my children were and they were going to come home and clean up the mess.

I re-loaded the babies into the car and set off, the Urvan screeching up the road for another adventure. Somehow I got to the school quicker than usual…

I marched into the office and very politely asked why my sons were not out the front waiting for me? The secretary, looking a little intimidated, directed me to the tutor's office. He asked me to sit down. I told him the mess in my kitchen was more important than what was happening in the classroom. He calmly suggested that releasing six boys from school was more a reward than a punishment and having one take one for the team was a better option. I settled for the compromise. After all, I wanted them to suffer as much as possible!

On the way home my son tried to reason with me, saying how embarrassing it all was. I told him I just didn't care if people thought I was a crackpot.

Once when John was away, I had seven boys to deliver to football games, two girls to tennis, and a birthday party on the other side of town for my 13-year-old daughter.

I decided I needed some quality time with her in the car, so after the boys came home, I left the younger ones in their care and took the babies with me. I gave them plenty of jobs to do, like cleaning up after lunch, and doing the clothes washing.

And after their rugby game, they would be too exhausted to fight, surely…

We eventually arrived at an amazing house. The mother invited me in for a cup of tea, and I was tempted to stay as I was dying to go inside for a tour. But something made me feel uneasy about the young ones being in the care of the rugby players. I kissed my daughter goodbye and began my return journey.

Driving into the driveway my heart skipped a beat. There was a mix of soil, ferns and broken terracotta pieces all over the driveway.

My pot.

Slowly and with great trepidation I carried the babies out of the van and opened the garage door that led to the playroom. The carpet was strewn with dirt and broken pieces of clay. With a baby on my hip and holding tight to my toddler's hands tears welled in my eyes as I plodded up the staircase into the kitchen.

There was food all over the table, dirt on the floor.

Where were my little ones? That was my main concern. I couldn't find anyone.

Suddenly before I could even ask "What on earth happened here?" The jersey-clad brutes came down the hallway and started flinging accusations at each other like the dirt that was all over the floor.

The one with the fiery temper confessed that his brothers made him so angry he tried to hit them with my large terracotta pot from the front balcony as they were running down the driveway.

We were one bad throw away from another funeral and dealing with the police.

It was one of the few times in my life I was speechless. I let go of any concern for the pot plant, the carpet, the messy kitchen. I ran the bath for the babies and was tempted to run it for myself, close the door and pour myself a glass of champagne.

Perhaps due to the gravity of the event, the boys worked hard to clean it all up, pay for the pot, and most importantly, apologise. So, despite all the chaos, there was no extra punishment that day.

With punishments it doesn't so much depend on the incident, but the attitude. And sometimes the incident itself is enough punishment, as the reality of what could have happened hit home with that heavy pot hitting the driveway and cracking into pieces. That crazy son also learnt a valuable lesson about self-control.

And I was quietly satisfied that I wasn't the only crackpot.

7

The Ministry of Labour

Our children would sometimes tell me that the only reason we had so many children was because I needed so many jobs done! I asked them "What came first – the chicken or the egg?!"

In his maiden speech to parliament, one son said he learned how to work hard by packing lunches and polishing shoes by the dozen. He said he changed 1,200 nappies in winter and then changed them again in spring! I guess that's poetic license... Surely as I'm the only one in our family to claim such a feat. He also said I took the term 'working families' to a whole new level. He's right there. Outsourcing and delegation – two essentials of management, can be practised right within the family home. Boy did I make use of some handy cheap labour. The thing is, it wasn't always reliable.

That's the problem when you outsource – the next in the chain of command can adopt the same policy. With a large pool of siblings at their disposal, their talent for outsourcing became too creative. A task entrusted to a 12-year-old somehow found its way into the portfolio of a pre-schooler due to some complicated backroom deal. The result was jobs poorly done, children projecting blame and wasted time. In the end, we had to pass a law ruling out job-swapping. They would have to find other avenues to exercise their talents in deception and manipulation.

Kids who tended to lose patience were given the task of listening to a sibling read; someone who tended to be selfish was asked to spend time with a sibling playing cricket; someone who didn't pay attention to details taught a younger sibling to set the table or fold the laundry into the correct baskets and so on. In this way, I seized control of the factional labour power-brokers and in the process kept an eye on quality control – not just of the work being done, but of my children's characters.

As a young girl I remember peering over a rickety fence watching our neighbour's kids have afternoon tea by the side of their pool. The picture stayed in my mind and I was determined my kids would have a similar afternoon experience. When they came home from school, butterfly cakes, choc-chip cookies, milkshakes or meringues and doughnuts were waiting. This became a family tradition that the children looked forward to, but it also gave us a chance to sit down and talk with a bit of peace and quiet as they filled their mouths.

Each afternoon after school, and more games in the backyard, the workers assembled to behold their duties, listed on the whiteboard hanging on the kitchen wall.

The whiteboard was the central organisational hub of the house. Even on the rare occasion I wasn't there to greet the kids when they came home from school, their jobs written up in bold ink on the whiteboard, were there to greet them instead. The whiteboard held a commanding position right above the afternoon tea table, so no one could plead ignorance of their tasks. Laundry was folded into baskets and returned to bedrooms, school shoes polished, lunch boxes delivered to the kitchen for a top up for the next day's feed, dinner prepared, and homework done.

Every second weekend after sport, it was on to mowing the lawns, sweeping the driveway, cleaning the pool, vacuuming the rooms, and cleaning the bathrooms. Everyone had a job, no one missed out, even the toddlers. In fact, the young ones have a much higher capacity and interest in household chores than the teenagers.

And only after all the chores were done, and done properly, were they rewarded with their father's overcooked BBQ steaks or their mother's mouth-watering-tomato-sauce-dripping hamburgers, followed by some fun in the pool.

There was always one who I had to constantly keep an eye on – he found work hard. In fact, he found it hard to do anything he was asked.

One Saturday he refused even to start his job of sweeping the driveway, let alone finish it. To avoid an argument I compromised and gave him the whole weekend to finish the job. A risky, longer deadline, giving him plenty of time to play and irritate his brothers and sisters. He loved taking risks and living on the edge. He also loved devouring his hamburger or chewing his tough steak, and playing in the pool with his hard-working siblings, who weren't exactly impressed that he had collected his wages before completing his job.

And of course he dared not work on Sunday, the Lord's day of rest. His problem was that in trying to avoid the Lord's wrath, he provoked his mother's.

On Monday morning he came bounding into the kitchen all ready for school. His perfectly knotted red and navy striped tie was pushed up against his crisp white collared shirt. He even managed to put his knee length shorts on the correct way and found those elusive garters for his long navy socks. His hair was slicked back off his beautiful angelic face and he was all ready for a hearty breakfast before leaving for school.

This guy was out to make an impression.

"Where do you think you are going?" I asked.

With his chest puffed out and a beaming smile on his face, he replied rather confidently, "School, of course."

"Oh, no you're not my love. You're not going anywhere until your weekend job is done."

He was in shock.

I told him he would learn more in one day at home fulfilling his obligation to the family than one day at school learning how to read.

When my daughters and daughters-in-law told me they rarely ironed clothes, I felt a little resentful, and tempted to feel I had been a mat for people to walk over for the past four decades, considering how many hours of ironing I had done. Then I realised that those hours of ironing were part of my professional work and I was right to take pride in the fact that on the whole, my children looked good and I taught them to have dignity in how they presented themselves. But I couldn't always do the ironing. One day I passed by my 12-year-old son, who was busy ironing school shirts and I said, "You will make a great husband one day, and your wife will be so pleased I taught you to iron!"

He turned to me and said, "I am never getting married. It's too hectic for me!" And he never did!

The job description for the school lunch portfolio changed over the years. Sometimes we were more socialist and centralised, with one person deciding what everyone would get and at other times, we were more free-market and decentralised, which could be chaotic but led to less argument. There was a lot of cling-wrap and greaseproof paper, but it wasn't foolproof. One morning the kids hurried off to school via the fridge, grabbed their colour-coded lunchbox and ran to the bus stop. In the afternoon, our eldest daughter came home very upset about her lunch. "Was it really that bad?" I asked. "You got the same lunch as the others".

"No I didn't," she retorted, opening her very heavy lunchbox to reveal last night's dinner leftovers – a huge serving of potatoes!

I couldn't stop laughing. Somehow she didn't see the funny side of it.

Despite being so concerned about food, kids cared little about clothes. After a while I refused to purchase any school uniform replacements if they were lost. The kids would just have to cop the detention and school punishment if they didn't have the right sweater because they lost it. We just didn't have the money, and besides, what message does that send?

It took time to come up with the most efficient system to distribute clean laundry but despite that, the kids sometimes just didn't comply. Every kid had a basket-like drawer in the laundry but they were often overflowing. Really how hard is it? All the washing and folding had been done. What else did they want? Me to go to each room and put it all away?

Well that wasn't going to happen. I wasn't their maid.

After a few warnings I told them to take their clothes baskets and if they didn't I would throw them out the windows and onto the lawn. Whether it was the front or back lawn depended on my level of annoyance. To this day I do not understand how they thought picking up clothes off the lawn was easier than taking their baskets from the laundry to their rooms. Our garden never really had a lot of colour until it was adorned with bright frilly undies, spotted socks and lacy bras hanging off branches. I also collected clothes off the bedroom floors and shoved them into plastic garbage bags and either threw them in the garage or gave them away to charity. It's amazing how often the kids didn't even notice some of their clothes were missing.

The rigorous industrial relations atmosphere in our home prepared our children for life in the real world. In fact, I think some of them were relieved to find less political working environments once they left home. They certainly had the confidence to stand up for themselves. One son had a job at the fast-food sandwich outlet. He would complain about how the mangers treated him like a slave and how the pay was pathetic. There had to be a better job somewhere out there. One day he arrived 15 minutes early and sat outside, observing that no one was waiting in line and it was a quiet day. When it came time for him to commence his shift he went in and started cleaning the bread trays. The manager moaned that it had been incredibly busy and they hadn't had time to clean. As a result, he needed to wash 50 or more trays. Then he was told one of the trays he cleaned wasn't done properly. Knowing they hadn't been busy at all, and totally fed up with the manager's pettiness, he removed his hat, untied his apron, and threw it on the floor. He told the shocked manager he was quitting. And he walked out.

Three weeks later he was working at another store with fairer managers. Other children went for jobs at KFC, McDonalds, supermarkets, delivered pamphlets or just took their musical instrument down to the mall to busk. Two sons helped the local milkman deliver milk in the afternoons, having the time of their lives jumping on and off a slow-moving truck and running back and forth leaving milk on doormats and collecting money. Those local jobs as young teens helped them get better jobs later on as they already had work experience outside the home.

But what most employers will never understand is just how paltry that experience was compared to their experience of work in the home.

8

Eat and Compete

The greatest solution to getting children to the dinner table, fed and out of there without too much disaster was to turn it into some sort of competition. Oftentimes a competition was the only thing to lure them from the backyard or pool or gaming device where another competition was competing with my competition.

And the best way to keep their minds occupied and their mouths full was to not just have the food ready but a whole set of quiz questions prepared.

We covered prime ministers, presidents, countries and capitals, and we had special ways of remembering them with sound associations. You can only guess how they loved to remember the capital of Bhutan – Thimphu…!

I fired questions at them from behind the kitchen counter as I prepared dessert. My teaching instincts told me they'd comply with instructions if they knew there was a chance of a treat if they got something right. Whoever was sitting up the straightest with the best table manners and paying the most attention was asked the first question. If they answered out of turn or interrupted one of their brothers or sisters they missed a go. In this way, they learned to respect one another, have a little patience, listen even when they knew the answers and learn a little humility.

As the children grew older and learned to read, they took turns researching articles in newspapers and journals on political and social issues. However, as time went on I compromised allowing a sporting article to be discussed once a week. I even learnt a thing or two about sport and it felt good to learn something from my kids.

One of the articles read one night was about parents bullying referees from the sidelines in an under 10's rugby game in Queensland. This fueled a very interesting family discussion. What poor examples these parents were to their children and to the game. It had become such an issue the media gave it a name – the Ugly Parent Syndrome.

One Mother's Day while waiting for the grandparents to arrive for lunch the boys called me into the dining room to listen to the radio. They were crazy about rugby league and listened not only to the commentary of the game, but the hour of analysis beforehand. From time to time they even called in to speak with one of the famous broadcasters, mostly out of desire to be given some kind of prize, like a supporters' T-shirt or jersey of their favourite team. The discussion turned to Ugly Parent Syndrome and they wanted people to call in and give their opinion. The kids insisted that it was my turn to speak to Ray Hadley, the radio commentator. I picked up the phone attached to the kitchen wall, near the back door, with my kids waiting with excitement in the next room to see if mum's call was picked.

"And we've got Anne on the line, hello Anne!"

I told them I had seven sons who played rugby and was shocked by the behaviour of these parents and the damage they were doing to the reputation of the game. I think they were shocked that I had seven sons. I was too scared to tell them I also had five daughters...

After I made my point we had a chat about large families and how much fun it all was. Out of respect and perhaps a bit of pity and certainly great empathy for my efforts to raise a team of football players, they sent me a generous voucher for the local liquor store!

These dinnertime discussions were beginning to pay off.

John also shared many stories about his business adventures to the Pacific Islands and sometimes even lands further away like Mongolia and Albania. The kids were always keen to hear about what it was like in the countries they knew the capital cities of but had never been to. One summer afternoon a colleague from Papua New Guinea came over for lunch. He was extremely engaging and knowledgeable about the issues and concerns of his country and region. And of course his skin colour made all my young white children sit up and take notice.

While waiting for the steaks to char we chatted on our back verandah watching the kids bowl cricket balls along on the dusty cricket pitch, where there used to be beautiful green grass. Others were playing Marco Polo in the swimming pool. The aroma of sizzling onions, steaks and sausages wafted through the air drawing the kids to the table.

Over lunch our visitor described in graphic detail the gruesome adventures he had while leading his clan in tribal warfare. The children fell silent, slowly lowering their forks and dropping their jaws as this man described the injuries he inflicted on others during battles and then turning up to work the following Monday in a suit and tie.

I felt a certain sense of uneasiness come over me as I was torn between being polite and protecting the innocence of my children. Then he invited one of our teenage sons back to his country for a trek! My son was so enthusiastic I had images of him dressed up in war paint with a machete in hand charging toward the enemy...

Only a couple of years later one of my sons did go to Papua New Guinea to help some very poor villagers by fixing their houses and school. I am sure John's work in the Pacific Islands shaped the way our children think and sparked their interest in humanitarian work and being open to other cultures.

One night, we gathered around the kitchen table listening attentively and patiently as each child spoke about their day. It all seemed quite dignified and controlled. But lurking beneath this picture of tranquility was an angry nine-year-old hungry for his voice to be heard...

He was struggling to talk over the clamour when suddenly he exploded into a vitriolic outburst. He complained that he was born at the end of the family surrounded by sisters while his brothers were born among brothers. They played cricket, rugby, went to a boys' club and even studied together not to mention having jobs delivering newspapers. He was too young to be included and it just wasn't fair.

As dinner continued and my indigestion intensified his face grew redder and redder and his voice louder and louder until all 12 pairs of eyes gazed at him. He went into barrister mode thumping his fist on the table pointing at each brother accusing each one of not spending enough time with him and his sisters of teasing him.

I watched his fiery eyes dart reproachfully from one sibling to another fearing where this was heading. We were shocked with this unexpected explosion of emotion. Just when I thought his father and I had escaped his wrath he drew breath and repositioned for his next onslaught. Leaning forward he slammed his hand on the table and bellowed, "You call yourself parents?" First it was John's turn for a dressing down. He was accused of spending too much time travelling and neglecting his fatherly duties.

Then turning to me with his eyes filling with tears he complained that I spent too much time studying. If only…

His siblings' looks ranged from confusion to amusement. The older children muffled their laughter and thought it to be very entertaining. One daughter even placed her camera discretely on the table and filmed the whole thing. The stunned younger ones sat in silence wondering how John and I would react. We sent him calmly to his room to cool off.

After we quelled the smirks, laughter and witty comments, we discussed how the boys could make more of an effort to play sport with him in the afternoons and the girls to stop teasing.

I went to his room a little later on, complemented him on his rhetoric, and told him one day he'd make a great barrister. It was obvious that he had been mulling over this for some time allowing it to fester into something bigger. I pointed out that in the future it was important to deal with situations before they become problems by speaking about his worries before they escalated.

The dinnertime forum was extended to school when the children entered debating teams and public speaking competitions. John and I would train them up and prepare them for their performances and on many occasions they came home with trophies in hand. One son now regularly debates in what they call the 'Bear Pit' – the Parliament of New South Wales, another is in front of the TV screens and radio microphone, one is an actor and director and others are practicing lawyers, marketing specialists, a stock broker or in the medical field - whatever they do they are all very capable presenting themselves in public.

And somehow in the midst of all that they even found time to eat.

9

Read-a-thons and Marathons

19 May 2016, was a very special day for me.

The marathon was over.

It was my last day of driving children to school since my eldest child started kindergarten in 1984. After 28 years it was all over.

All of it.

Cross country races; athletic and swimming carnivals; music lessons and performances; basic, advanced and instructor survival courses; Easter hat and book week parades; debating; public speaking; mock trials; afternoon training at the local park; making lunches and butterfly cakes for afternoon tea; cleaning school shoes; ironing and mending school uniforms; making garters; finding silver buttons to re-sew on boys' blazers after being pulled off in a school fight or lunchtime footy game; sewing little blue buttons on girls' summer uniforms; mending holes in winter kilts made by compulsory kilt pins; trying to keep impractical white summer hats clean; mother/daughter camps; coaching basketball; backstage crew at musicals; part-time teaching; class parents; parent-teacher interviews; parent functions and arguments; Higher School Certificate preparation; presentation and speech nights; graduation dinners and luncheons; snow trips; and sports games.

Long before deciding what schools to send our children to, I taught them how to read and do maths at home using the Glenn Doman 'Words and Dots' System. It was based on word recognition and memorizing pages of red dots ranging from one to a hundred. I decorated the kitchen walls and windowsills with these pages and at breakfast, lunch and dinner they would practice reading the words and memorizing the number of dots. Gradually they progressed onto simple readers then novels expanding their vocabulary, broadening their knowledge, deepening their understanding and stimulating their imagination. However, not all our children were avid readers and a couple needed a little extra encouragement. Over time bribery became the order of the day and they made some solid progress as they approached the ripe old age of five.

They were not too young to start. And not too young to learn virtue and good use of time. As a result, they took primary school in their stride. For secondary school, it was more up to them, but our rhythmic recitations of the mathematic times tables in the Urvan on the way to school was the first lesson of the day, and to be honest, I think most of them were relieved to get out of the van and get into the classroom for a bit of a break.

I struggled getting one of them to read at all. He just wasn't responding the way the others did. I remember thinking 'What's wrong with him?' He took longer to understand some simple primary school concepts. I started worrying about his development and decided that school just wasn't up to the task with him. How would he grow up and get a job if he got left behind? I decided I would homeschool the 10-year old. It was a frustrating year.

I would teach him the times tables but his eyes started glazing over and his attention waned. What was I going to do? Eventually I started giving in by allowing him to watch movies. But I insisted he watch classic ones such as Robin Hood and Black Beauty. Gradually he became interested in books based on stories from the movies. He could now visualise the characters and make sense of the plot. I would get him to read while I was cooking dinner and I'd watch him mimic the facial expressions of the characters in the book and imitate their voices. He was an entertainer. I realised this kid just had a very different way of learning – and had different skills and tastes from my first few children. That difficult marathon of a year was coming to an end and I was almost disappointed he would return to school.

During our home schooling year I realised he was a visual learner and was excellent at expressing himself orally. When he returned to school I asked his science teacher to test him verbally. The teacher obliged and the result was 98%! This kid was smart!

Today he is on stage doing improvised comedy, writing movie scripts and producing, directing and acting in films!

I hope he doesn't resent that year at home, and that he eventually enjoyed our lessons. I certainly learnt the lesson that some kids learn differently from others.

We had high expectations of our children's schools and their teachers, but over time had to realise that they, like our kids, were never going to be perfect. I also had to detach myself from my children's day-to-day concerns. In fact, experiencing difficulties during those school years provided many opportunities for them to learn appropriate strategies to respond. And that skill was key for their future jobs, marriage and social relationships.

But sometimes, they did need a helping hand, particularly when my maternal instincts took over. On special days such as birthdays the children were given extra treats such as chocolate in their lunch-boxes. One day one son came home upset explaining that a bully in his class had stolen his treats. I complained to a friend who instructed me not to send treats to school. Was she kidding? Why should this oversized bully curtail my son's freedom? No, we needed to be imaginative to send a clear message home to this bully.

I waited, just a few days. Then I sent some more chocolate treats to school in my son's lunch-box, adding a special one wrapped in brightly coloured tin foil. When my son opened his lunchbox at 'little lunch', the bully overshadowed the scene and my son very meekly handed over the special chocolate. The towering bully grabbed it and shoved it into his mouth, smearing his face and laughing triumphantly. But this really was a special chocolate – pharmacy laxatives.

Needless to say our bully didn't spend much time in the classroom for the rest of that day.

It's not the modern way of dealing with bullies, I'll admit. But my son wasn't bothered again, and hopefully learnt how to use his imagination to get out of a tight spot.

At times we didn't agree with rules and policies at schools, and found them too prescriptive and inflexible, but we learnt, along with our kids, that rules need to be respected, and perhaps the kids didn't need to be embarrassed by mum and dad complaining.

But honestly.

One school rule required parents to make appointments with each subject teacher to discuss exam results – as the teachers kept the exam papers for the following year, so they didn't have to come up with new questions. At the peak we had nine children at school, which meant meeting 54 different people to go through exam papers. Seriously?

That's when I got in trouble, for asking my daughter to sneak her exam papers home. The kids loved it when I did something wrong like that – we had an understanding between us and we bonded through being accomplices. The teachers must have hated us.

So did the neighbours.

I wanted my kids to play musical instruments – we had the guitar, the violin, the trumpet, saxophone and piano. Evening practice was extreme, and we had little concerts from time to time that I quickly regretted as some kid ended up fighting over the triangle and the conductor stormed off in a rage. One neighbour was rather difficult and had two dogs that would bark and bite every time one of the kids accidently kicked or threw a ball over the fence and tried retrieve it. When they thought the dogs were asleep or inside the neighbour's house they would straddle the fence and slide down the other side to reclaim their property. Once over, they discovered she had a store of their balls in her outdoor shed. They were shocked at her meanness and began to develop a payback plan by practicing the saxophone and trumpet in our cubby house that was right next to her kitchen. I am sure we became the neighbours from hell!

From time to time we had been asked by schools to take on some responsibility and organise things for the families in a particular class. Early on in our parenting career, we poured our efforts into family fun days and exhausting events, coaching sports teams, and as the years went by we were happy to see other younger families take up the mantle. However, it wasn't fair that our younger children missed that kind of input from their parents, and so every now and then we picked up the mantle again to coach a team or get involved in events. One of our daughters was school captain and so we organised the senior formal.

It was like organising a wedding.

Thankfully, John was working from home and could help with organizing this event. I'm not sure he got any other work done that year – maybe that's why he started looking for a new job!

He made an excel sheet itemizing the costs of the venue, seating preferences, menus as well as documenting payments. Besides designing and sending invitations, decorating the venue and tables, organizing a class photo to adorn the massive cake, I had a huge learning curve creating a slide show with music depicting the girls' schooldays from kindergarten to year twelve. I also needed to organise security, and a hundred and one bits and pieces to ensure the night was a great success.

On the big day I dropped my daughter off for her beauty treatments telling her I'd be back to pick her up in a couple of hours so we could prepare for the pre-formal drinks we were hosting. One of the good things about offering to host the pre-drinks was that our kids pitched in and cleaned up the house and garden in preparation for the big night. After dropping her at her appointment I charged across town to the venue to set everything up. I put up the screen for the slide show, sorted out computer problems, ran from table to table and checked the place cards matched the table list I typed up at 3am that morning!

Time was running out. My daughter rang from the salon wanting to know where I was. Where am I? How am I? Stressed and having issues with the computer. I sped back across town picked her up and drove home to prepare for our guests. My children were amazing as the house and garden were perfect and they were organizing trays of food as I walked in the door. I only needed to give out a few more instructions and get ready for the night. It was all so hectic.

It was another marathon, and we were almost there.

But we were so caught up with all we had to do, I hadn't realised John was looking pale, breathing heavily and slowing down.

He was having a heart attack.

After all his stories to the children about Pheidippides and the Battle of Marathon, he was about to do the same and arrive at the destination and drop down dead!

So John didn't make the formal that year, but thankfully we got him to hospital in time and he was looked after very well.

In the end, the night was a hit with only a few complaints about seating arrangements and the amount of wine on the tables. I remember thinking these parents were expecting miracles, while I had a husband in hospital. We had an awesome night dancing late into the evening and toasting the graduates. And sending photos to John in his hospital bed.

Another child through school and on to her next adventure. Another marathon run.

We were very lucky to have a school that took mentoring so seriously. We would meet with 'tutors' and discuss issues our kids had, in a constructive way. They took a real interest, but at times a mother's protective instincts bristled and reacted to the feedback. Once we were told that one son was uncoordinated and shouldn't bother making too much of an effort in athletics and sport.

That was like a red rag to a bull.

The cross-country competition was coming up, and a new regime was about to begin.

I would collect the children from school and head directly to the local park to train.

I prepared snacks, drinks, had their joggers ready in the van and I joined in to push them along like a drill sergeant. John helped me make a list of warm up exercises. We would have afternoon tea and then they would start their running, pushing themselves for an hour and a half. I remember being 7 or 8 months pregnant running next to the preschoolers encouraging the older children to run faster while I timed them doing laps around the oval. Next, they had to run up and down the grassy hill on their toes lifting their knees higher and higher as I shouted, "Do you want this???' "YES we do!" "Do you want to win?" "YES we do!!!" "Come on you can do it, feel the pain, remember no pain no gain! You've got this, go PERROTTETS!"

Our so-called 'clumsy son' was getting fit. Very fit. The big day arrived, and John, a successful runner himself, took the day off work. He was in the van giving them last-minute tips:

"Make sure your shoelaces are done up tightly".

"If your shoe falls off just keep running". (Really?)

"Remember it's a pack start. It will be crowded and there will be plenty of pushing and shoving. Keep your distance so you don't fall over. Take your time to work your way into a good position towards the front of the pack. Keep a steady pace throughout. Remember your breathing and your rhythm. When you move toward the leader make sure he feels your panting breath and the thudding of your feet so he knows you are right there. Unnerve him by continuously moving closer and then falling back a little so he loses his rhythm – but don't pass him just yet. With about 200m to go, start your sprint. Go straight past the leader in one swift move keeping a good distance in front. Don't look back, don't finish with anything left, just focus on crossing that finishing line first!"

I felt exhausted already!

On arrival John took up his position near the finish line and I stood further away, up on a balcony with a better view, holding my heavily pregnant tummy, and praying.

He needed to win this race.

The gun went off and they shot off, my son was somewhere in the mess of moving bodies and scrawny legs pounding the ground. They disappeared in the bush and down the back of the school, appearing and reappearing every now and then but too far away for us to see. It felt like an eternity, or at least like another pregnancy.

Suddenly, I saw a small indistinguishable figure appear, coming up the crest of the hill and crossing the field. As he edged closer I could see he was sprinting. Was this our son? Please God, please, let this be our son. The goose bumps spread over my body as I looked for the signature Perrottet legs and running style.

It was a match! The lone runner on the field, bolting now towards the finish line with a triumphant and confident style was our son, way ahead of the pack. I wanted it all to slow down and the Chariots of Fire music to play.

I was so proud. It was the most satisfying marathon of them all.

Tears filled my eyes as I watched him run across the line and up into his father's arms. John lifted him high up on his shoulders in victory. His face was so red from the heat and the exhaustion of pushing himself to the limit. Beads of sweat trickled down his forehead, around his eyebrows, dribbling onto his panting triumphant chest.

He went on to win many more races in school and beyond, play cricket, rugby, and lots of other sports.

No one tells my children they can't do something.

However, I'm not sure I would have reacted and pushed my children that hard if I hadn't heard those words from that skeptical teacher.

Maybe he knew what he was doing.

10

Birds, Bees and Penguins

Naively, I thought all my children would sail through life at the same speed.

But I realised many of them were in very different boats, going at different paces. Except of course when they got into trouble and I'd punish them all together saying "You're all in the same boat". It was so much easier that way. All for one, and one for all.

But I did have to learn that not only were they not in the same boat – sometimes they were in a completely different ocean.

Some were more like their father – cool, calm and collected, but possibly bottling up their emotions, while others were more like me – extroverted and expressive, perhaps a little too much at times!

Driving bumper to bumper up the long driveway at my daughters' school, my eyes scanned groups of girls sitting in the pick-up line waiting for their ride home. I was impressed how the teacher on duty always smiled as she waved cars along the queue reading off family names positioned clearly on dozens of dashboards. I often found this rather stressful though, as I feared being distracted by a crying baby; a toddler choking; a bag caught in the door; or a school note that needed to be passed in and missing my wave along. As I inched further forward' I noticed one daughter sitting on the grass staring blankly across the school oval with a forlorn look on her face. When the girls hopped in the van, I asked the usual questions: "How was your day"? "What did you do at lunchtime"? "Did you miss me"? and so on. On this particular occasion, I received a monosyllabic response from a forlorn looking daughter who was normally quite talkative and jovial.

Silence filled the car on our way home.

The little snacks I baked during the day for afternoon tea couldn't even put a smile on her face. I suggested we go for a walk. She was quite willing to get out of the house and away from everyone for a while. We walked down the street in silence. I held her hand from time to time and gave her little hugs as I encouraged her to share what was on her mind. I knew if I asked her straight out I wouldn't get the whole story. We kept walking and chatting as the afternoon sun warmed our backs until we arrived at a park and sat down on the grass next to the swings. As she pulled at the blades of grass and tore them into little pieces tears began to roll down her cheeks.

There was a problem at school with a girl in her class and she wasn't sure what to do.

I asked her how her friends felt and whether she had told any teachers. She said she had but nothing had changed. It was actually getting worse. It dominated lunchtime conversation and everyone was becoming rather negative as a result. I asked whether she wanted me to intervene in some way, as John and I had a leadership role among the parents that year. She declined the offer wanting to work it out for herself. So as we walked along chatting we brainstormed and came up with a few strategies she could try. Our joint problem solving worked and the situation eventually resolved, and many lessons were learned. I explained that girls her age can be rather emotional and reactionary rather than thoughtful and measured - actually most females can be I joked, just look at me! I also advised her not to become ensnared in gossip as it will only make matters worse. The important thing was to be positive and look for solutions. Hopefully, that was not too much advice as I think it important children try to work through their own problems with a little guidance when necessary.

In the same week, another daughter arrived home from school clearly upset. So off to the park we went to tear up more blades of grass.

But this time it was different. Before we even reached the opposite side of the road she dissolved into tears. She told me she was really upset with her sister, who she found bossy and condescending. I suggested they talk it over together. She was not keen – she wanted me to fix it. We chatted for a while as I gave her some suggestions on how to approach her sister. The most important thing was not to take sides but help her to communicate in an unemotional and mature way. They were so different in temperament. However, she needed to learn how to deal with conflict and what better place than in the family. I have always told our children that they have been blessed to be part of a large family where they can find many opportunities to learn when to speak up and when to shut up!

John doesn't mind me saying that, one of my life projects is to get him talking about emotional matters. However, as the passage of years have passed he is sharing many more thoughts and feelings – one of the treasures of growing old together.

Our neighbour, Col was a lanky, kind and friendly old man who lived right across the road from us for many years. He had the years of worry edged across his brow and walked with his back slightly bent. His wife, Sheila, was bed-ridden with an infirmity we didn't know about as we rarely saw her, and only spoke to Col when he was tending his garden. They also had four adult children who had long moved away.

Col clearly took great pride in his garden. His immaculately manicured lawns were the envy of many a bowling green. Petunias and azaleas shadowed by red gum trees graced their expansive corner property. Often I would see Col walking around admiring the fruits of his labors. One day I walked across and asked how he kept such an amazing garden.

"It's all Sheila actually" he said.

Strange, what could she have done in the garden?

He pointed to her bedroom window.

"Through that window Sheila can see everything – a panoramic view. She's mapped out where every flower-bed should be and where every tree should be planted."

Col was her hands and feet and she was the mastermind behind such an amazing spectacle of bloom.

In contrast, our front garden was a mix of dry, brittle grass that crunched under your feet as you walked and dusty brown dirt patches where the basketballs or cricket balls landed. Over the years I tried cultivating a few garden beds and even planted a lush rain forest down the side of the house. However, it didn't take long for them to be desecrated by kids chasing after balls or each other or stray rabbits they brought home devouring every carefully planted fern or palm. I eventually succumbed to our property either being used as a cricket pitch, footy field or a basketball court depending on the season.

The problem began when the backyard grass had been so pulverised that the kids needed a new, more hardy cricket pitch. And they were sick of losing tennis balls over the fence to the neighbour's dogs. So, the

Perrottet Cricket Board made a decision to relocate to the front yard. There would not be so much 'turn' on the concrete driveway cricket pitch, meaning batsmen were hard to get out and the balls were being hit everywhere. Including the beautiful outfield across the street – Col and Sheila's manicured front lawn.

Sheila not only oversaw Col's gardening prowess as she peered through her front bedroom venetians but also a foreboding presence of tennis balls. She dreaded the cricket season. On occasions she would send Col over to tell our kids to keep the cricket game on their own property. We could tell Col felt uncomfortable doing this but to keep him from Sheila's complaints the children tried to oblige. However, their resolutions did not always play in Col and Sheila's favour. One hot summer's day they whacked the tennis ball for a six down the pitch, across the road, over Col's lawn missing those precious garden beds and onto his roof nestling into a section of his gutter. Relieved it had overshot Col's garden the kids found another ball and continued to play.

It wasn't until we had a rare downfall of rain that Col appeared at our front door, soaking wet, holding a tennis ball in his hand. The ball had lodged in the gutter and the result was a waterfall inside their house!

One day when the boys were out the front playing cricket again I noticed an ambulance pull up in front of Col's home. I just had a feeling that it was serious.

I went around the side of the house and beckoned the boys to stop playing and come around the back. I just assumed they would follow the instruction and obey. Back inside, I watched closely what was happening across the road from the lounge-room window. There were two paramedics moving Sheila out to the ambulance.

She was covered in a sheet.

And my boys were STILL batting the ball down the drive towards the ambulance!

Furious, I ran down the back stairs, around the side of the house, pushed open the side gate and told them in no uncertain terms to come inside. I don't know if it was a shouting whisper or a quiet yell. They were totally oblivious to what was going on around them.

"Why didn't you come in when I told you?" I asked.

"It's only an ambulance," they replied. "And we were hitting the ball up the street anyway".

"Boys! Sheila has died. The way you boys hit the ball you'd probably hit one of the first responders or worse…Sheila!!"

A few days later I suggested to John that we take a meal over to Col and extend our condolences. He agreed. Before we ventured across the road I sought reassurances from John that he would at least say something so I was not the only one doing all the talking. He agreed. I was skeptical. John was not always the best communicator especially when it came to things of the heart.

So across the road we went and knocked on the door. Col didn't answer at first so John went to turn, suggesting we leave the meal on the doorstep and I go see him during the week.

"Let's just wait a little longer".

Col eventually opened the door and greeted us warmly and invited us in for a cup of tea. I realised I had never been inside Col's house as he showed us into his 60's style lounge room with floral patterned lounge chairs and matching carpet. While Col went to the kitchen to boil the kettle I gave John an encouraging look to be sure he spoke up and passed on his heartfelt condolences. He gave me a reassuring look back. Somehow, I wasn't convinced. We sat down and chatted for about an hour as Col talked about Sheila and what they had accomplished in their life together. I asked questions and Col opened up. It was beautiful and moving listening to him. Eventually it came time to leave. I hugged him, John shook his hand and we made our way back across the road.

"Oh, John" I sighed.

"What?" He asked.

"You didn't say a thing!" I lamented.

"Yes, I did" he retorted.

"What did you say?" I quizzed.

"I'm sure I said something like, I'm sorry for your loss."

"We were there for an hour and that is all you could say, five words, 'I'm sorry for your loss?'"

"You two seemed to be doing just fine without me adding anything more!"

What more could I do other than accept that everyone communicates in different ways and I am sure Col appreciated John just being there to listen to his love story.

Over the years I have learned that males communicate differently to females. When the children were younger and I wanted John to chat with one of the boys, I'd suggested they go for a drive. In this way, the conversation could bounce around from engines, to rugby, to John's job, to their schoolwork without making eye contact and eventually land on the topic that needed to be attended to. This seems to work best.

When the children were younger they loved asking questions – nonstop like most kids. One son in particular was very curious about the impending birth of our new baby and kept asking when and how he would arrive. They assumed it would be a boy as having a girl appeared to be a slim option!

"How is he going to get out of your tummy, mummy?"

I used to enjoy putting the question back to them. He told me he thought it would come out of my tummy button. Then I let the cat out of the bag and told him the baby comes out through a special opening in my body… But I don't think he quite understood.

"Oh, does he go down some stairs?"

One of my daughters at the age of five became even more curious about how these little babies kept coming into our home and asked…

"So how does the baby get inside of you?" It was just too early for that, but before I could come up with a response, she said to me, "Oh, don't worry, I know mummy. You have used up five babies already and now you only have 20 more left inside you"! She was so content with her own answer I left it there.

The real crunch came when she was eight or nine. Sitting together on her bed in her room I explained everything. I recall her not being too shocked by what I said and wondered if she really understood. In the end, I repeated 'The Talk' a few times over the coming year to ensure she got the facts in a healthy way rather than on the bus or in the school playground.

One day I was driving home from school when one son asked, "Mum can I ask you something"? "Sure" I replied. "Well at school today the boys were laughing at a word in a magazine but I didn't understand what was so funny". "What was the word, I asked"? "Orgasm" he replied. Well, I began to imagine a group of boys gathered around a dirty magazine down the back of the school and thought I was going to be in for quite a conversation. I very calmly enquired, "What was the name of the magazine?" "Amazing Facts" he replied. I raised my eyebrows and slowly nodded my head and asked what the magazine said? "It said that penguins only have one orgasm a year." I had to hold back my laughter as well as my relief. I told him that I felt sorry for penguins! "Mum, why do you feel sorry for the penguins?" He asked.

"I'll explain this another day, darling!"

When our girls were young and wore pretty little dresses I encouraged them to pull their dress hems over their knees and sit as elegantly and as modestly as a little lady could. I thought if John and I could nurture in our daughters the importance of respecting their bodies it would put them in a stronger position to resist the lures of their world. Any parent will tell you that it certainly gets harder as the children approach the teenage years, especially the girls. One morning one of my daughters came out of her bedroom wearing a rather short dress. I asked, "Where do you think you are going in that young lady? And by the way where on earth did you get that dress? Or is it a top?" She responded, "Your standards are just too high". I paused then gesticulated with my arms, "OK, where would you like me to hold the bar? Here or here?" She answered in a surrendering tone, "Hold it there, mum", pointing to the higher arm.

Believe it or not, kids actually want rules, standards and boundaries; they know they need them and they want direction – they need an anchor to pull them back if or when required.

I am proud of all my children, but I melt when I tell the story of our youngest son's generosity and business acumen. He is extremely hardworking, focused with an amazing amount of energy, fortitude, and resilience. As a result he raised almost $30,000 for volunteer projects while at school and university and with his own funds has contributed to the needs of the family especially when times have been tough. That's love with deeds, and it's his way of saying he loves us.

At thirteen years old he organised one of his usual chocolate-selling events, which always surprised us – in terms of how much chocolate people are willing to buy. He is probably responsible for half the neighbourhood and his classmates if they contract diabetes. But this time was different – there was no volunteer project or obvious cause for the fundraising and we were starting to get suspicious.

Months later, John arrived home from one of his business trips, on the day before his birthday. My son told him that the next day they needed to go for a drive.

So they did. John got in and drove the car and our son drove the agenda. He had the map, the instructions on how to get where they were going, and John had no idea.

Half an hour later they pulled up at the shops and got out.

As they walked along, they slowly came to a stop in front of the 'Pro Golf' shop.

As they entered the salesman walked over and asked, "What can I do today for you fine gentlemen?"

John explained that his son was the customer.

Turning to our son the salesman said, "Hello young man. How can I help you?"

"I want to buy my Dad a birthday present" he said. "Certainly!" Came the reply. "What is your price range?"

Standing tall with his chest puffed out he said: "A thousand dollars!"

John was speechless. "You have what!?"

"I've got a thousand bucks," he repeated nonchalantly.

The salesman's eyes lit up. "Well, that will take you a long way in this shop."

John asked, "How did you get that much money?"

"Selling chocolates."

Still dumbfounded, John followed the salesman passed the single club displays, passed the economy brands and toward the 'state-of-the-art' golf clubs! Once John made his choice, our son did all the negotiating.

As they arrived home, we all ran out to greet them. They opened the boot. Our jaws dropped in disbelief as they revealed a huge black leather golf bag, containing a full set of golf clubs, balls, tees, a golf glove, and even socks for the club – the whole enchilada! It looked awesome. Our son had decided that John's old wooden clubs which had been handed down from his father, needed to go.

I felt tears coming to my eyes to see his generosity. "What's next with you??" I asked almost rhetorically.

"A boat – so we can go fishing together."

Years later most of the children pitched in and bought John his boat. And once again we're not all in the same boat, as it's a one-man kayak.

But still, he does call it his 'boat'.

11

Nintendo Swims and Artificial Limbs

With the school term over and the kids sleeping in I found myself sitting alone at the kitchen table gazing out the window wondering what to do with them over the holiday break. I wanted the holidays to be fun not only for the kids but for me. I had children of varying ages with differing requirements. The older ones wanting to spend time with friends; the younger ones happy playing with their brothers and sisters and the babies needing their sleep. Trying to balance everyone's needs was a real challenge.

One day after the kids had played all morning, we had 'quiet time' in the afternoon when the little ones slept and the older children read and did extra schoolwork. It was in that window of often-interrupted peace that I stole some time to pray and read. Both children and parents need holidays to recover mentally, emotionally, and physically from the rigors of the school term and take time out to rest and enjoy family life, but that doesn't mean weeks and weeks of not doing any work. I enrolled them in holiday programs where they could do sport, a bit of work, and something creative to keep their minds and bodies active as well as meet new friends.

Sipping on my tea as I gazed out the kitchen window that morning, I wondered how I could make this holiday period a little different to the others. Strumming my fingers on the kitchen table avoiding the spilt milk and scattered cornflakes I found myself looking at the telephone books sitting on the kitchen bench. White pages for residential and yellow pages for commercial phone numbers and addresses, there was no 'google' back then – only phone directories.

As I walked toward the kitchen bench to pick up the yellow pages, memories of a school excursion to the Coca Cola factory came to mind. Dressed in school uniforms and looking rather regimented, the class assembled outside the school where the buses were waiting. We were only going to the next suburb but we were so excited. As we reached the factory I craned my neck out the bus window trying to get a clearer view of the huge bottle of Coca Cola on the factory roof. Once inside we were given white caps to cover our hair and were mesmerised by the enormity of the place. Clinking glass bottles weaved their way on conveyor belts like long, dark snakes. Each bottle was filled, labeled, and packed and on its way out the door. I remember being fascinated by it all.

As a family we visited museums and galleries from time to time when they gave family discounts – but we weren't in the habit of visiting theme parks and movies all too often as we just couldn't afford it.

I put down my tea and began my search for an activity that didn't cost an arm and a leg.

Naturally I started with A and 'let my fingers do the walking' as the Yellow Pages advertisement went. Before long I came across the Artificial Limb Factory.

Wow! Artificial limbs!

I picked up the phone – the ones that used to hang on the wall – and punched in the numbers. An elderly gentleman answered. I explained my situation and asked whether they conducted tours of the factory. He spoke quietly and compassionately asking whether a family member was an amputee. "No", I replied. "I just thought it would be interesting and educational for my children to see how artificial limbs were made". He was rather surprised yet happy to organise a tour. In fact, he told me there was a museum displaying an extensive history of the development of prosthetic limbs that the children may be interested in.

We had about seven children at this stage ranging from twelve to a few months old so I needed some help. I rang a friend and convinced her that this would be an awesome experience. She hesitantly accepted this unusual invitation. Now all I had to do was convince my kids that this was a cool way to spend part of their holidays. Convinced or not they piled into our van and we drove to an inner-city building.

The gentleman who spoke to me on the phone greeted us warmly and directed us down the corridor toward the glassed-in room that was used as the museum. With hands and noses pressed up against the windowpanes the children were guided through the history of incredible feats in the making of prosthetic limbs. As interesting as this was they were even more intrigued by what happened next. An elderly gentleman with long grey trousers approached them as they were lined up along the hallway. He asked whether they could pick which one of his legs was artificial? Always ready for a bit of competition the bets were on! He paraded up and down the hallway like a fashion model on a catwalk. Mind you I was checking out his legs too! The bets were as even as his gait. He was brilliant and we just couldn't tell which leg was fake.

After the correct trouser leg was lifted to reveal the prosthesis, and the winners declared, we walked past a group of people in an exercise area complete with small bridges, steps, gravel, grass, and pavements. People of all ages were holding onto railings as they painstakingly walked up and down stairs transitioning between different levels and surfaces trying out their new limbs.

Next was an exercise room where a young girl was struggling to hold up her body as she inched along the parallel bars. On closer inspection she only had a few fingers on each hand and was missing a foot. The determination on her face was remarkable, something I will never forget. We continued with our tour and followed our guide into the plaster room where an eight-year-old girl was having half a foot prosthesis fitted. She was laughing as she joked with the technician. Her father had accidentally ran over her foot with a ride-on mower when she was just three years old.

My kids were starting to become quiet and pensive.

My seven-year-old son was a little confused by what he saw in that plaster room.

"Mum, why was that little girl laughing when she only had half a foot?"

"Well you don't need a whole foot to be happy. Happiness comes from deep within when you live a good life and try to please God. There is only spiritual and bodily perfection in Heaven, I'm afraid."

After a long but extremely interesting day we arrived home exhausted and ready for baths, dinner and bed. As I cooked dinner on our large brown double oven I noticed the brand name, St George, written in italics under the temperature dial.

What a great idea.

The oven factory wasn't half as interesting as the artificial limb factory.

However, the glow from the huge furnace the size of a small room used to heat metal sheets certainly enflamed the kids' curiosity. After a while we moved on from this glowing inferno and were directed toward the assembly line where men and women painstakingly separated nuts, bolts and screws. As we passed one of the kids very honestly aired his thoughts.

"How boring must that job be!"

On the way home in the car we had a little talk about the importance of and respect for all types of work. I explained that as lowly as they may consider that job to be it has more merit if done well than a well renowned doctor, lawyer or politician who does their job poorly. The merit is in the effort a person puts into their work not in the prestige of the job. I asked what they thought of my job staying home raising a family and not getting paid? Or performing well at school only in subjects they liked or only with teachers they got along well with? I told them it's a lack of good character and virtue if we don't give our best in all things, regardless of the excitement level or the pay.

In between excursions to factories and other activities I sometimes left the older children in charge of the younger ones while I ran a few errands in the morning. The holiday plan as usual, was that they do their chores before watching TV or playing on the Nintendo 64.

On this occasion I wanted them to get up, get dressed, make their beds, tidy their rooms, have breakfast, clean the kitchen and put on the laundry washing before I returned home. There were certainly enough of them to spread out the workload over the hour or two I was away!

I returned home within a couple of hours to find nothing done.

And in these holidays, it was becoming a habit.

They hadn't even got to the first, basic task – they were sitting in their pyjamas playing Nintendo.

I was cranky and frustrated and I needed something new and extreme to get my message across. Somehow that year, the kids were paying far more attention to the Nintendo than my instructions, and their dexterity with the consoles was exceeding their ability to turn on a washing machine.

There could be only one solution. It wasn't the Nintendo's fault, but it would feel the full brunt of my anger.

With adrenalin pumping at high speed through my veins, I ripped the plug out of the wall, grabbed the machine, stomped up the stairs, threw open the kitchen door, stormed onto the back verandah and with a deep breath heaved it across the backyard, over the fence, and into the swimming pool.

It felt so good!

It was exhilarating watching it sail through the air, across five metres of lawn and splash! Into the pool it went, sinking slowly to the bottom.

I was impressed with my effort.

The kids, not so much.

Now, if the first miracle of the day was my record-breaking throw, the second was that two of my sons, who had previously fought and fought over whose turn it was on the Nintendo, forged an unlikely bond.

One of them dived, like me, fully clothed, into the pool to save his baby, while the other ran for the hairdryer. This was winter in Sydney, a little chilly and definitely too cold to swim! The image of the two of them standing shoulder to shoulder bonded by a single mission was impressive and even emotional… what brotherhood!

Unfortunately, there was a third miracle that day – they managed to fix the Nintendo.

12

Breaking the Rules

One spring evening just as the warmer breezes started to arrive and the smell of the blossoms down our street gave great encouragement that summer was nearer, I opened the playroom door leading to the garage to find my youngest children sitting in three big red canoes on the garage floor – life jackets on, oars in hand, they were excited, but going nowhere quickly.

Every year in one of the holiday breaks John would take the older children on a trek. Their goal was to complete the entire Great North Walk – a 250-kilometre journey from Sydney to Newcastle, John's place of birth. It's a well-marked track that snakes its way through the bushland around Sydney's north-west suburbs before straddling the Hawkesbury River and working its way up to that old city made famous by the BHP steelworks.

But this time was different. They decided they would break the rules and instead of walking half the designated leg, they would canoe along the river. My children were so excited, especially those little ones who hadn't realised yet that they weren't going.

I had a few basic rules about holidays and one was that I didn't go camping. I wasn't intending to break it this time. I was always very happy to stay at home with the young ones while John heroically set out with the older kids, hoping to bring back the same number he left with. Spring was a good time to do it, because the days were long enough to make sufficient progress before the real heat of summer arrived with fire bans and the risk of dehydration. They had to carry everything on their backs including food, water, sleeping bags and tents. And this time it was complicated by John's great plan to shift from bush-walking to canoeing.

In the evenings after the younger ones went to bed John and the older children, ranging in age from about 10 to 13 years, studied the maps and examined the terrain, plotting the best stopover points to replenish supplies. The trip began with an overnight walk from our home in Pennant Hills through the Galston Gorge to Crosslands Reserve on Berowra Creek on the upper reaches of the Hawkesbury River. This is the traditional land of the Darug people. The Darug people are a group of indigenous descendants who survived as skilled hunters. They have a strong sense of community and kinship and today live in family groups or clans mainly in Western Sydney. I hoped the spirits of the Darug people would protect our motley crew by teaching them their traditional survival skills and sense of kinship! I had a motherly instinct they may need their help on this trek…

They were accompanied by some close family friends, while their mum and I were tasked with a special job of meeting them at Crosslands for lunch on the second day and to drop off the canoes that John had tied onto the vans before leaving.

We provided a scrumptious lunch for our intrepid explorers just in case it was their last! We spread the picnic tables with plastic tablecloths laden with chicken and chips, bread and tabouli, some drinks and a few chocolate biscuits. After loading up the canoes with supplies and passing out last-minute instructions the captains ordered the crew to board for their three-day expedition to Brooklyn. We hugged them goodbye and wished them well. The younger children stood along the bank in the shadows of the huge gum trees and weeping willows whose elegant leaves swayed in the waters of the Hawkesbury. They shed a few tears as they waved their siblings and friends goodbye.

Brooklyn was near the mouth of the Hawkesbury River, which joins the Pacific Ocean at Broken Bay, the major waterway north of Sydney. Our beloved explorers spent their days drifting along with the current while the captains taught the children to master their canoeing and navigational skills. They were fishing and singing songs and entertaining each other with riddles and puzzles. The first evening's campsite was atop a steep cliff overlooking Calabash Bay, not far from Berowra Waters marina. It was many metres above water level, so they tied up the canoes and used a rope pulley system to pull their bags up to the flat landing.

They passed the time sitting around the campfire toasting marshmallows, telling stories and praying the family Rosary before retiring to their tents for the night. Being a strategist, my husband assigned age appropriate jobs to everyone such as clearing the campsite; collecting firewood; boiling water; preparing meals; pitching tents; organising equipment; setting up lanterns; and securing canoes.

The second night involved a much easier approach as they moored on an uninhabited island and set up their tents, eagerly expecting a short journey around the bend to Brooklyn the next morning, where we would be waiting with the cars and the younger kids.

But not so quick. They could tell in the morning that the weather had changed, and as they shifted their sore bodies back into the canoes they could also tell the water was not so peaceful. The river had widened by now and as they turned the bend and emerged from the protected part of the river, the wind picked up and started throwing the choppy water into waves. They were blown off course into the middle of the broad, fast flowing river. The canoes took on water and some of the younger kids were losing control, risking capsizing and losing their belongings, if not their lives.

The dads had to make a call and helped to steer the canoes to the shore where they took refuge in a mangrove swamp. Their shouts and calls for help died down as they realised they were safe enough, but they were still a long way from Brooklyn Bridge, which was only a blur on the horizon, through the squally wind throwing rain in all directions.

From Brooklyn, we stood at the edge of a platform overlooking the river, but we could hardly see anything through the gale, and were worried about their delay. We climbed to a craggy outpost to get a better view of the river bend hoping to catch a glimpse of our intrepid explorers. The wind was getting stronger, whipping up the waves as well as our concerns for the safety of our husbands and kids. Meanwhile, we were given some relief and consolation when we noticed the coast guard keeping watch from the other side of the river.

The river along the muddy shoreline was quite shallow and the dads were able to tie the canoes together, preventing them from being separated. With ropes stretched over their shoulders, waist deep in water, they dragged the canoes along the shoreline, with choppy water hitting the sides of the canoes like the scene from 'The African Queen' with Humphrey Bogart and Katherine Hepburn! The children either sat in the canoes or walked alongside trying not to get their footwear bogged in the mud.

Time was ticking by and we were starting to get emotional. Slowly, three miniscule red dots on the side of the river came into focus, and we wondered and hoped it was them. We began waving our brightly coloured scarves, hoping to catch their attention giving them hope that it was not much further until they would be safe and sound again on terra firma. As they pulled ashore we wasted no time running down the boat ramp embracing them and checking they were all in one piece.

I immediately introduced a new rule – no canoeing. Only bushwalking. In fact years later, they returned to walk that leg, just to say they had walked the whole journey.

Each of these incredible North Walks had their own unique challenges. One spring it had been particularly wet leading up to the trek. As a consequence, there was an abundance of leeches, snakes and ticks. Everyone was on watch against these deadly predators, especially the leeches. They are amazing creatures that will burrow, in the slipperiest sense possible, through clothing and shoes, to get at the skin and suck the blood. Their natural anaesthesia prevents you from knowing

anything is going on before you see it and fall into fits of screams while
someone else tries to rip them off. John always carried his trusty 'Medi-
swabs' which worked like magic. On this particular trip, after a good
deal of the rain that John had promised would stay away, it seemed they
had arrived in the middle of the national leech convention. The blood-
sucking creatures were out in force and had generated a sense of panic.

Suddenly a scream for help echoed from the front-line. Rushing
forward my husband found one of the girls with a leech burrowing into
the webbing of her boot and not long afterwards another child had a
leech burrowing into her shirt. In no time these blood-sucking creatures
generated a sense of panic.

At one point one intense son was in a state of half undress, with his
foot standing in a plastic container to avoid all contact with the natural
environment, and he starting screaming: "It's a leech, get it off me, get
it off me!!"

His siblings rushed to his aid, but couldn't find the offending leech.

"Get it off, get it off, it's right there!"

He was hysterical.

And after a careful search they pointed to the black basketball shoe
on his foot and asked whether he was looking at the small black loop you
grip to pull on the boot.

He stopped screaming.

But his siblings haven't stopped reminding him about it. He had a
particularly frantic approach to any kind of insect that might invade his
room as he was growing up.

These encounters with nature reinforced my determination not to
join in those rigorous character-building treks. However, over the years I
learned 'never say never' because before too long John finally convinced
me to join them for one leg of the walk. As a consequence, I broke my

golden rule and went camping.

It would be fine, he reassured me as the spring rains weren't all that threatening. So with a certain amount of trepidation but with an optimistic disposition on my part we drove to a camping spot in an idyllic setting canopied by gum trees with a creek ebbing and flowing over rocks below. We pitched the tents, ate dinner, toasted marshmallows, told stories and prayed the Rosary. This was really enjoyable but I was getting tired and a little preoccupied about getting kids settled in tents and planning the trek for the next day.

As uninviting as the tent looked, I just wanted to crawl inside and sleep. I had a thin air mattress and couldn't get comfortable. If I lay on my side my thighs hurt while if I lay on my front or back I couldn't sleep. But at least the kids were in their tents and it was 'lights out'.

Suddenly I heard an almighty shriek from the kids' tent. We army-rolled out of the tent, got up and rushed over. My son was screaming that there was a massive insect trying to unzip his tent! After a close inspection we realised it was a moth that was magnified by the light of the moon casting a shadow on the outside of the tent wall. We settled him down assuring him nothing or nobody could get into his tent and attack him. Finally, he calmed down and we turned to crawl out.

Just as we opened the flap of his tent, there was a clap of thunder, the heavens opened and raindrops the size of grapes smacked us in the face. Mud, slush and I don't even want to think what else splattered up against my legs as we trudged our way back to our tent. Drenched and uncomfortable, I cleaned myself with whatever I could find and settled back onto my wafer-thin air mattress to sleep.

Before drifting off to sleep John told me that if the rain continued we might have to call the trek off.

I told him: "I'll pray. It will be OK."

I prayed for more rain.

I woke up an hour or two later as I needed to go to the toilet. My husband, ever the gentleman, guided the way with his torch. We walked down the hill trying to avoid the cow patties. Pushing the rusty old corrugated iron door open I feared a spider or two might run up my arm, or worse. I held the torch close as I lifted the toilet seat with hands covered with toilet paper. I don't know why, but I shone the torch right down into the pit. I wasn't sure what was worse, the sight or the stench.

Why was I doing this?

I am not a camper. I'm a horizon pool lady, longing for hot spas and resort living. I should never have broken my rule.

"For the family, for the family." I kept repeating it to myself. I had to prove to them I could do it.

I slowly made my way back up the hill to crawl back into my half-star canvas lodge and somehow got back to sleep.

In the morning I woke to the most beautiful sound.

Heavy, torrential rain.

The tents were leaking and the backpacks drenched and our expedition was terminated.

How hard I tried to act disappointed. I suspect John knew my prayer intentions that night but he didn't say anything.

I haven't returned to a tent since. As I said, I'm a resort kind of person.

With John travelling so much to the islands for work, there was the odd occasion I was able to go too. This provided me with some well needed rest and recreation. Once we took the whole family on a holiday of a lifetime before the older ones started leaving home.

We stayed at an island resort in Fiji's Mamanuca islands with warm tropical waters that were so clear, and colourful fish darting around the kayaks and surf skis. It was truly a paradise. Before long I abandoned my shady seat on the beach and found myself on a Jet-ski.

The water was pristine, the sun was beating down, and I burnt out across the water in my water motorcycle, hitting the maximum speed as quickly as possible. The warm tropical wind filled my soul with exhilaration and freedom as I jetted away from the demands of family life. I remembered that we shouldn't just wait for bad times to talk to God, so in my peaceful solitude I thanked God for the trip and the opportunity to see such beautiful scenes.

The jet-ski was secure and I felt safe, as I flew partly on the water, partly above it, and turned, veering around the small island. By this stage I might have been half-way around. I was lost in thought and a million miles away from everyone.

An approaching patrol boat suddenly awakened me from my euphoric state. The captain flagged me down and called out that I was a long, long way from where I should be. Apparently it was against resort rules to go beyond the beachfront. I was a long way from the beachfront. I was on my way to another island! As I had come so far, he allowed me to continue to circumnavigate the whole island and return that way. It was an epic journey of freedom and I didn't feel a single pang of guilt. The reprimand was worth every exhilarating moment.

Sometimes breaking the rules means you end up swimming in a tent, other times you're leading a Fijian patrol boat in the open ocean like James Bond. Knowing when to break them and when to hold firm is a fine art.

13

Blood and Water

The arrival of our 13th child on my birthday, 1 June 1998 was an unexpected treasure. In the first trimester I threatened to miscarry. My doctor advised as much bed rest as possible. This was not going to be easy as the house was undergoing renovations to accommodate this new addition and I had eleven other children to chase after! Conveniently, John had to attend a tourism conference on board a cruise ship in the French Polynesian Archipelago.

The perfect place for me to rest!

I had my bags packed in no time and organised the children to stay with our friends while we took off to the South Pacific for a week. Thanks to the South Pacific Tourism Organisation the pregnancy continued without a hitch.

Most of my babies were born a couple of weeks late so I was determined that number 13 was going to come on time and arrive on my birthday. One day someone suggested I try castor oil as it brings on labour! Why didn't anyone tell me this before? As a result, three times a day for three days before the baby was due I forced myself to swallow two tablespoons of castor oil followed by gulps of milk to deaden the taste. That's an indication of how desperate I was to deliver this baby on time. With a fair amount of trepidation I pinched my nostrils tight, tilted back my head and spooned the oil slowly into my mouth. As it slid down my throat my head shook in disgust, my jaws tightened and my teeth clenched as I tried to stop myself heaving after every disgusting sip of this toxic liquid.

Hoping the castor oil would work its magic I went to bed every night with my bags packed dreaming I'd have a baby in the morning but nothing happened. On the evening of 31 May I watched a sad movie called, 'Nicholas' Gift'. A story about a little boy who was shot and killed and his parents donated his organs to another little boy with a heart condition. A beautiful movie, a real tearjerker stirring my emotions that perhaps brought on a few mild contractions. Paying no heed to these teasers of pain I turned off the light and tried to sleep. Laying in bed feeling sorry for myself I suddenly felt one strong contraction and thought my membranes broke.

No, this can't be happening. I always get induced.

My membranes never break without assistance so this is just a false alarm. I turned on the light, sat up and rested back against the pillows. Those teasers of pain were becoming more regular and stronger so I headed toward the bathroom. Passing one of the teenagers in the hallway I asked him to find his father. With the renovations in progress the only working bathroom was the ensuite in my eldest daughter's bedroom. I sneaked in trying not to disturb her when she whispered, "Are you okay?"

Within seconds John came bounding in after running up the stairs and bellowed breathlessly, "Hey, the children told me you were having the baby!!" "Not right now!" I explained. "But we need to go to the hospital soon or our van may become the delivery van!"

When I returned to my room to get my bags I passed a large clot of blood. This was scary and so very different to the other births. Something was wrong. I began to worry as the contractions were becoming stronger and more frequent. We gave the older children instructions on what to do during the night if the kids woke and assured them John would be back in the morning to help with the school routine. Fearing a home birth our two eldest children carried my bags quickly to the van, opened the garage door and encouraged us to hurry up. Backing out the driveway I will never forget the relief on their faces as they stood in the garage and waved us goodbye.

Driving along the Comenarra Parkway to The Seventh Day Adventist Hospital at Wahroonga the contractions were coming at an increasing pace but were bearable. Thankfully it wasn't peak hour so the traffic wasn't too bad and we managed to get there in good time. We drove up to the emergency parking area where John helped me out of the van and rang the emergency bell.

The staff seemed to take ages to answer.

Straight to the delivery room I went, grabbing the happy gas along the way. All was going well until one huge contraction arrived unexpectedly. Whoa! I usually built up to this intensity of pain but this time was so different. The pain had well and truly arrived, but my doctor hadn't. The urge to push overcame me and by this stage I didn't care who was there and who was not. They told me to wait or I would tear, so I waited, but not for long as with one push our little baby was very quickly born … on 1 June 1998.

I asked what sex the baby was but no one replied.

I asked again and still no answer.

The silence reminded me of when Joseph was born. I began to worry.

Eventually they handed me my beautiful little baby girl and I was overjoyed. Strangely, a certain amount of tension filled the room. The nurse instructed me to put the baby on my breast immediately and start feeding. Slowly I realised there was a problem, not with the baby but with me.

I was hemorrhaging.

The midwife massaged my tummy to help the uterus contract while another nurse caught the blood in a container then poured it into a measuring jug to monitor how much I was losing. The doctor who never missed a birth arrived just seconds later and was briefed about my condition. He took over the massaging. His fist was big and strong and his massaging was painful. I put my hand on his to stop him but he explained he needed to do this to help the uterus contract. But nothing was working.

With all my babies he delivered I never saw him look so concerned as he did on this day with lucky number 13! I started to feel extremely weak, but peaceful. I turned my head to the right and saw John holding the baby on the other side of the room away from all the action and only could communicate with our eyes.

More and more people entered the labour ward as the atmosphere intensified. The doctor asked for a drug to be injected into the Syntocin drip that had been put up earlier. It was not effective. They couldn't stem the bleeding. Blood was everywhere, spilling out of measuring containers onto the floor and down nurses' scrubs. It was beginning to look like a MASH unit. The doctor called for some blood in case I needed a transfusion, as the hemorrhaging was not subsiding. It was the era of the HIV scare so I was worried about receiving contaminated blood and asked if John could donate his. I was told there wasn't enough time – it was either donor blood or die.

The pathologist came and took a sample of my blood to cross match the blood type. A few minutes later she returned saying she didn't get a good enough sample. My doctor appeared irritated and told her to take what she needed for a better match. There was certainly plenty of blood to go round! However, so much was going on with limited access to me she decided to do what she could with what she had. She returned with two half-litre units of blood, as that was all they had and even then it was not the exact type but it was at least compatible. The doctor rigged up the blood bag to get the transfusion going but the pump wasn't working. Becoming increasingly frustrated and annoyed he asked for a replacement pump and a blood warmer as they didn't have time to warm the blood. Cold blood running through my veins was a very strange, almost horrid feeling.

While all this was going on a nurse was constantly massaging my tummy. I became extremely thirsty and whenever John could get near me he gave me sips of water and ice to suck on. Whenever they stopped massaging there was another gush of blood. The second unit of blood had been exhausted and another two were put up. When the pump was being changed some bags of blood spilt over the floor, on the bed and of course I was already covered in it.

Over the years, John had regularly fainted at the sight of just a small amount of blood. To this day I don't know how he managed to stay upright!

The room was bursting with people by this stage from the delivery team, to pathologists, to the intensive care team and other doctors. I was not improving and I had now lost over four litres of blood. The doctor then told me he needed to inject a drug directly into my uterus.

I can still feel the needle.

It was odd shaped and very long, and he pushed it straight through the walls of skin and moved around until he found my uterus and injected the drug. Apparently, it was a new drug and a rare procedure and he needed to be extremely cautious not to damage the surrounding organs. The pain was intense. I looked toward John for reassurance as we had hardly spoken throughout the whole ordeal. He knew what I was thinking, "Hey, what's happening?" "Am I in danger?"

The doctor continued pumping the blood while the midwife monitored the amount of blood loss. Slowly the drug seemed to be taking effect. After some time the doctor moved toward John and reassured him I was going to be okay. However, if this drug had not worked the doctor would have needed to perform an emergency hysterectomy.

After the injection took effect I became delirious and vomited feeling quite distressed. It was now 3am, an hour and a half after delivery. They took the baby from John's arms to the nursery to have her vitals taken. They repositioned my tubes and lifted me from the bloodied delivery bed to a clean, crisp white bed trolley and moved me down the hallway to the Intensive Care Unit. They also wrapped me in a type of bubble wrap heat blanket called a 'bear hugger' to raise my body temperature because of all the cold blood I had received.

The Intensive Care Unit was very quiet with dimmed lights and people speaking in hushed tones. The doctor told John I had lost such an enormous amount of blood it would take me a very long time to recover.

It took me two years.

Still hooked up to the blood transfusion bag I was able to self-administer the morphine whenever I felt the need. I was floating! What a feeling! Between sucking on ice and self-administering morphine, I was in heaven. John was by my side through it all then left about 6am as I was drifting in and out of sleep. He went home via the nursery to cuddle and take photos of our gorgeous little girl.

So now I had all the time in the world to reflect on what had just happened. Just about dying from blood loss was a rather peaceful experience. At the height of all the activity back in the labour room I felt a spiritual presence. I felt Our Lord and His Blessed Mother standing beside my bed and Our Lady said, "Anne, you are doing a good job". This was so reassuring and to this day I remember Her words especially when I think I'm not doing such a good job.

Over the years I have come to realise that God doesn't want my perfection but my love and my desire to improve every day. The merit is in the struggle.

If our van wasn't delivering me to hospital to deliver babies it was delivering our kids to emergency to get stitched up, glued together or pumped out after some disaster. No matter how much we tried to keep our kids safe it didn't always go according to plan. One Saturday afternoon a teacher from our boys' school came over to discuss their academic progress and school behaviour. The conversation ended abruptly when the soccer game that was happening in the backyard became a little too competitive.

The teams were unevenly matched from the beginning with our youngest son in one team competing against a couple of his older brothers in the other. They were kicking one of those huge lime green tennis balls the size of a soccer ball when out of the blue the youngest son who was losing by a country mile kicked the ball between the upright posts of the clothesline, scoring a perfect goal. Out of breath and in a euphoric frenzy after scoring such an impressive goal he ran toward the ball enthused for another goal. Feeling sorry for this younger brother doing it alone one of the players on the winning side decided to swap teams to even up the odds. Sometimes an act of kindness can backfire and backfire it did when he gave him an encouraging shove through the goal posts impaling his head on a rusty nail protruding from the side fence.

More blood.

The impact hadn't given him a massive cut but we needed to go to the hospital and get him stitched up. Thankfully, his head was glued back together rather than stitched and he was back on the playing field in no time.

I don't know what it is about Christmas but someone always seems to end up in hospital. In the summer holidays the kids were working in the garden mowing, trimming hedges and cutting back trees in preparation for Christmas. Our 17-year-old son had the job of trimming the hedges. After finishing he headed toward the garage to return his tools, wash up and get ready for lunch. Unbeknown to him his 19-year-old brother was lurking in the darkness on the other side of the garage preparing to pounce. Ignoring the fact that the younger brother was carrying a pair of large hedge-trimmers the older one charged full pelt into him pushing him over the back of a nearby couch and onto the cushions. They lay there wrestling for some time until one let out a blood-curdling scream, which was followed by a stream of blood.

It was the older one. Just desserts.

John called for an ambulance. One of our daughters relayed the answers back to John who was fielding questions from the paramedics. "Is he breathing?" "How much blood is he losing?" "What colour are his lips?" and so on. Eventually the ambulance arrived just as the bleeding began to subside. He was taken to hospital and glued back together.

One son in particular could have done with a whole pot of that glue.

By the age of thirteen he had broken several bones – five in the space of 18 months! He broke his hand playing the first game of baseball for the season; broke an ankle and a leg on separate ski trips; broke both elbows at one time trying to scare a few of his siblings by leaping from behind the toy cupboard door, jumping over a lounge and landing awkwardly on the carpeted concrete floor; broke a toe kicking a rock; broke a wrist and another toe playing sport; and was then attacked on a footpath by a pack of pit bull terriers and needed multiple stitches.

But perhaps nothing was more memorable than his ill-fated trek in the Blue Mountains. He was with 12 boys and two adults, attempting to complete their Duke of Edinburgh Award. About 7:30 pm one night we received a phone call informing us that half the boys had gone missing. The group had somehow split in the middle of the Jamison Valley and one half had made it back but no one had heard from the other half for hours.

We were extremely worried. People die from heat exhaustion and dehydration in those mountains. Our son did not have provisions for another night and needed his prescription medication.

John and another son decided to drive up to the area to join the search party. The police told them that no inexperienced hiker would be allowed to join. It was too dangerous.

Night fell, the search was called off for the day and all we could do was pray.

The next day the police agreed to bring in a helicopter. The waiting game continued as the helicopter circumnavigated the area for hours. Time was passing and the sun was beginning to set, again.

We felt helpless.

The boys had left the track because it was damaged and steep and they were intending to join it again, but in that dense scrub, you can so quickly lose your way. They were fatigued from beating their way through the thicket and on their extra night out, they had reached an outcrop and could see the cleared clifftop and lookout where the track ended. They decided that in the morning they would aim straight for it, but it wasn't going to be easy.

They were tired, and very, very thirsty. No one had extra water.

They had lost clothing, had run out of food long ago, and after a day of trekking, they had settled close to a sheer stone wall at the base of the valley to catch their breath. One of the boys in the group suggested building a green fire and sending smoke signals, and it was this that caught the eye of the circling helicopter rescue crew.

They hovered low and directed them to the track – only metres from where they were. It proved that despite their amazing navigation to get where they needed to, it was still so thick they hadn't realised how close they were. One of the boys had a mobile phone, but they explained it had run out of battery as he had been playing games on it on the first night before getting lost.

They stood there in their torn clothing, ashen faces, guzzling water and eating pies.

Their team leader who was feeling rather sheepish himself tried to turn the situation into an opportunity to learn something about hope, struggle and destiny.

"What did we learn, boys?" He asked rhetorically.

While they struggled to think of a response, he answered, "Shit sometimes happens".

Somehow, that profound phrase became the boys' motto. One of the boys had even carved it into one of the trees that he thought would be encasing their corpses. They had clearly bonded deeply through their ordeal. Blood is thicker than water, they say.

I say the Blue Mountains bushland is even thicker, but the thickest are those who decide to turn off the track.

14

Torn to the USA

One morning in 2012, I walked pensively up the stairs to our bedroom carrying the usual morning cup of tea and coffee. Tears welled in my eyes as I placed John's cup on his bedside table and walked around to the other side of the bed and slipped in. As I sipped my tea he began to stir and saw tears rolling down my face.

"What's the matter?" He asked in a drowsy voice. Through my tears I explained my worry over our financial situation and didn't know what we were going to do next. Propping himself up on his elbow he turned to me and placed a comforting hand on mine as we sat together in silence for a moment. John had been working for the World Bank but some years before had decided to go it alone and use his extensive experience to do some consulting. But the Global Financial Crisis hit, clients were far more conservative than expected and we were feeling the pinch.

He reached over to his bedside table and fumbled for his phone as he put on his glasses and punched in his passcode. Searching through his emails he eventually found one, looked at me over the rim of his glasses, and handed me the phone.

"Hey John, how are you going? Would you be interested in a job in Washington DC?"

I was shocked and speechless… well, for a few seconds.

"So are you going to accept the position? Yes? Great! Let's wake up the kids and go!"

John's more measured approach is often painful, but I know his wise and lengthy deliberations can often save us from my crazy ideas. But this crazy idea was an opportunity, in the land of opportunity.

And we really didn't have too many other options.

The next six months seemed to go in slow motion. My excitement about selling up and moving out to the other side of the world was tempered by the slow bureaucracy of the world's biggest development bank.

And even on the home front, the process was not easy.

I had imagined everyone sitting around the kitchen table, others tuning in on phones and computers as we made the startling announcement. I visualised the American national anthem playing, champagne corks popping and glasses filled to the brim.

But the only thing that popped was my bubble of naivety about how they would respond.

My youngest son was devastated.

"What? When? Before Christmas!?"

He was gutted and couldn't comprehend what we were telling him. He had aspirations of being school captain and on graduation night walking across the same stage his brothers before him had walked. He also had amazing friends at the school he attended. There was nothing we could do to console him. Over the ensuing months he had numerous offers of adoption. It was impressive just how many friends he had, how many parents loved him and how much he loved his school.

The married children and those well into their careers thought it to be a fabulous opportunity for us. And although it was a great opportunity, I knew I would not only miss my children but my grandchildren. I loved to spend time playing with them reading stories and taking trips to the park and very much looked forward to forming strong bonds as they grew older. And although most of our children had left home, we still felt responsible to provide the family home and host family functions.

We felt so torn. This crazy idea was going to cause our children and us a lot of heartache.

John left for the U.S. to start the job and find a house. Three months later he returned to Sydney and gathered us up for the big move. While he was busy in the U.S. we were busy packing the house. We held a garage sale, and ordered a shipping container, and I needed to finish my final year of study in psychology. Life was hectic but it helped ease a long, sad goodbye.

At Sydney airport on the morning of 16 December 2012, we dragged our bags along the airport floor, and my heart was dragging that low as well.

Kissing and hugging our adult children and grandchildren goodbye was very difficult.'

I felt guilty about leaving my nineteen-year-old daughter behind, but she won a scholarship to a residential college, completed her undergraduate degree; finished a Masters of Bioethics, did an overseas placement, got into postgraduate dentistry and juggled all this between two or three jobs. Then she decided to get married in her spare time! It really is amazing what children can achieve without their parents.

Another difficulty we had was saying goodbye to our old parish priest. While we sometimes tested his patience, he was a fabulous priest, a great friend and a fantastic role model for our children – especially our sons. He was faithful, dedicated and obedient with a fantastic sense of humor and an uncompromising and unshakable faith. He was completely at home with ordinary people and totally politically incorrect. When the Pope visited Sydney in 2008, he was the oldest serving parish priest in Australia! When asked if he would like to sit next the Prime Minister his response was "Why would I want to do that!?" As he grew older he sometimes forgot where he was in the liturgy but he never thought of retiring.

At the age of 92 he was admitted to a convalescent hospital. Before we left for the U.S. we all visited him to say goodbye and thank him for all he has done for our family. As we left, I kissed him on his forehead, as I knew I would never see him again. A nurse followed us out and asked why we were crying when only a few minutes before we were chatting and laughing. We explained he was not just our old parish priest but a close family friend who we were going to miss terribly. He baptised all but one of our children and buried one of our babies. The nurse assured us he was very happy to spend time with us, as he was known to ask other visitors to leave soon after they arrived!

It wasn't just hard for the kids. John felt sick with the risks he was taking as the head of our family. I knew I would miss being the matriarch of our large and growing enterprise, hosting luncheons; political functions; family celebrations; Christmas parties, and just being there for the kids and grandkids. Now I had to pass this onto other family members prematurely.

We arrived on American soil with our three remaining teenagers on 16 December 2012 to begin another crazy chapter in our lives.

The 22-hour journey was extended when we missed our connecting flight on our final leg in Los Angeles and ended up in Phoenix. We were greeted in DC by one of our sons who arrived ten days earlier. The August before our departure from Sydney he attended a short course at Princeton University. So with a taste of the States in his blood he decided to study his remaining Law units online and live with us in the U.S. for a while. I was overjoyed as this not only meant our youngest son would have a brother here in the U.S. but I would have another one of my kids with me.

Our trip through the streets of DC toward our home in Bethesda, Maryland was surreal. Was this really happening? Were we actually going to live in the USA? The unfamiliarity of the place was inspiring, the monuments majestic and the bridges were works of art. Before we knew it we pulled into the driveway of our new home. We opened the front door and were amazed at what we saw. It wasn't the ambience or the grandeur of the place but the Christmas decorations that took our breath away and made us feel right at home! Our son had recreated Sydney in Washington!

Then came the fearful first day of school for my youngest son. We arrived at school earlier than the others as there was a delay due to the inclement weather. The secretary suggested we go for a walk around the grounds and check out the gym. We walked along the winding sandstone path and met the coach. When he discovered we were from Australia his first question to my son was, "Do you play rugby?" Rugby was a relatively new sport at the school and the coach was keen to get a seasoned player on the team. By the time we left the gym my son was not only on the team but assistant coach! No matter what prejudice I had against rugby, it certainly saved my son's life that day.

There is no doubt in my mind the life-changing impact the coach had that snowy winter's morning. Being in a team sport provided a pathway to fit into the school community, meet some great friends and contribute on many levels. Over the three years he was at the school he embraced leadership roles at every turn running for class president, captaining the rugby team and receiving the 'Cavalier Award' for the player that demonstrated outstanding leadership, sacrifice and perseverance on and off the field.

But the first few weeks of training and practice games did not go well as the team fell short of my son's expectations resulting in a barrage of complaints from him about the team's level of commitment and talent. My youngest daughter and I began to dread picking him up in the afternoon anticipating the agonizing drive home listening to everything that went wrong in training. I told him he needed to think about the solutions rather than the problems. He was not that receptive, so I needed to think more creatively. After picking my daughter up from school one afternoon I suggested we take a slight detour to 'Subway'. She was quite happy to do anything to delay the afternoon barrage of complaints! After our 'sojourn' we drove along the tree-studded driveway leading to the boys' school, past the tennis courts and the pond where they skated when it froze over, then up the hill toward the rugby field where he was waiting. He threw his gear in the trunk, pulled open the side sliding door and hopped in. An aroma of gastronomic delights floated out of the car as we passed him a foot-long sub!

With his mouth full and his stomach satisfied he developed a far more positive attitude toward the team along with a few extra pounds but it was well worth it for the silence and for our sanity!

The other great challenge was navigating the seven lanes of traffic on the Interstate 495 – the highway between Maryland and Virginia. With my hands clenched tightly on the steering wheel, eyes riveted to the frenetic traffic ahead and knuckles turning white with fear I navigated the long expanse of the road, but at times it was just too much. Some days the snow would be heavy enough for the school to call a 'snow day' and cancel classes, but there were also a few times I called a 'traffic day' and my kids didn't make it to school.

One morning in March I woke up to the silence of falling snow. It was so beautiful, so white, and so soft. Coming from Australia this was a little piece of heaven! My mind began to tick over. I know it's March but what about a Santa photo in the snow? One of our many family traditions is to take a Santa photo where an important family event took place during the year, such as a graduation or wedding. However, we never got around to it the Christmas we moved to the U.S. Although I thought this was a great idea I had reservations about what John and the kids might think. However, within the hour we were all dressed in our Santa gear and ready for the photo shoot. John dressed as Santa with the whole suit – red and white outfit, beard, glasses, and boots, me dressed as Mrs. Claus in much the same outfit except for the beard and glasses and the kids in Christmas T-Shirts and hats. Only one thing was missing, someone to take the photo. By this time our neighbour Ken wasn't surprised with anything his crazy Australian neighbours did and gladly came over and took the photo for us. Every year we decorate our walls with our Christmas photos including the one we had taken with Ken. This is very special because that was Ken's last Christmas on earth.

The thing that is so striking about the U.S. is the size of the place, even for an Australian. We lost the kids at Macys once not long after we arrived.

We also had many Aussie visitors. On one occasion a good friend of our eldest son in the U.S. spent a few days with us. One afternoon they decided to go into DC for the night and meet up with friends. They were about 23 years old at the time. The next morning I went down to the basement where they were sleeping to see how the night went. The beds had not been slept in. I checked my phone and there were no messages. I rang his phone and there was no answer. I Facebook messaged him and there was no response. I began to panic. I woke the girls and shared my concerns. I rang the police. They asked for a description of what he was wearing. I was so stressed I couldn't think. The girls filled in the details. The lady on the end of the line told me they don't start looking for people until they have been missing for more than 24 hours. However, she had compassion probably because she was a mum herself and could hear the panic in my voice. She said there was a patrol car in the vicinity that they would send over.

In the meantime, our youngest son arose from his slumber and asked what the all the fuss was about. I explained that we couldn't find his brother and needed to pray as I had visions of him lying dead in some alleyway after been shot through the heart. It took me a long time to adjust to the fact that guns are legal in the U.S. At times my imagination got the better of me! He reassured me they would be fine because he just spoke to him! "What? What do you mean you just spoke to him? I haven't been able to contact him all morning!"

Suddenly, I heard someone call out from upstairs, "Hey, mum the police have just pulled up in front of the house. What will we do? Hide?" They asked. "No", I replied. "There is only one thing to do". "Get ready to take some photos of what I am about to do next". I opened the front door and marched toward the police car. When he saw me coming he opened the passenger window. I leant in and explained that my son who was lost is now found! He asked, "How old is your son, ma'am?" "Twenty-three", I replied. He paused, looked at me and said, "Ma'am, your son is considered to be a man not a child". "What? My children are always my babies no matter how old they get!" He laughed and we chatted about Australia and his connections with Adelaide and he gave advice about keeping the house safe and asked me if there was anything else he could do? "Yes, actually there is one thing, could I have a photo with you?" "Absolutely, no problem, Ma'am". I ran back into the house and called the children. "Quick, get your phones and take a photo!" They were mortified but obeyed and now I have this awesome photo of me with a member of the Montgomery County Police Force.

The Montgomery County Police played a significant role in our lives in the U.S. One day I was driving my older daughter to a modelling shoot appointment. We were following our GPS and turned down a road that was under construction. We passed a police car and slowed down. Before we knew it we heard sirens and were pulled over. My daughter gave me the following instructions, "Turn off the engine, get out your license, open the window, don't take your hands off the wheel as he may think you are reaching for a gun and by the way don't speak before being spoken to". Her advice didn't fill me with a lot of confidence as I didn't have a U.S. license and we had been in the country longer than the three-month period of grace given to international drivers. The policeman approached and spoke so quickly we couldn't understand what he was saying. He recognised my Australian accent and spoke more slowly. In the end, we started talking about Australia and how homesick we were and offered him accommodation whenever he decided to go down under. After a great chat he let me off without a fine and turned back toward his car. I told my daughter to lean out her window and get a photo of this upstanding Police Officer. Our photo collection is growing!

Our time in the U.S. has been incredible and has left a strong and lasting imprint on our lives and the lives of our children. By the time they graduated from high school they didn't want to go back to Australia. We all made lifelong friends; did a road trip across 'Route 66'; met up in Disneyland with some of our children and grandchildren from Sydney; drove along the Big Sur; biked across the Golden Gate Bridge; trekked through the National Parks and gave a talk on 'Communication in Marriage' at a family conference in Beaver Creek, Colorado. Believe me, a five-week car trip across the U.S. with my husband and a couple of kids taught me a thing or two about communication! We trudged knee deep through snow on the way to school; prayed for snow days so school would be delayed two hours or cancelled; completed ACTs and SATs – don't ask me what the acronyms mean; college applications and essays; defended theses; had senior joke day; school musicals; Graduation Ceremonies; Baccalaureate Masses and Award Nights as well as Junior and Senior Proms; mentoring students; snow trips; and learning to drive on the 'wrong' side of the road...

The USA was also the country I fulfilled a life time ambition –

graduating with a Bachelor of Arts (Psychology) and a Bachelor of Community Welfare and Counselling. Unable to work in the U.S. I volunteered as a student mentor at Oakcrest School for Girls in McLean, Virginia and later enrolled in a Masters of Applied Positive Psychology. Every parent needs to be equipped with tools to help them through all the inevitable ups and downs of life in a positive and constructive way.

Who knows where we'll end up. But one thing I am certain of is that God has an incredible plan for us. He will lead, challenge and encourage us and open our eyes to many amazing possibilitiies. It's a bit unsettling at times to think we are reaching retirement age and don't know where we will finally settle. I've moved homes so often in Australia and the U.S. which focuses me on where my true home is – heaven.

We felt so torn to leave Australia, but will resettle back there soon. We have made so many wonderful friends in the USA, and I fear we are going to be 'torn again'.

15

Keeping the Faith

I just adore Christmas. When I was a child the school term finished a few weeks before Christmas allowing time for shopping, decorating and cooking. Our artificial silver Christmas tree stood about four feet tall in the corner of our lounge room between the sandstone fireplace and the glass doors leading onto the front verandah.

The tree was decorated with gold and silver tinsel and colourful glass baubles hanging off several of the fragile branches. I loved decorating the tree and watching the presents grow as Christmas Day drew near. But most of all I loved building the nativity scene. I usually found a discarded cardboard box and covered it with aluminum foil and pulled apart cotton wool balls placing them on top, as clouds. Inside this humble abode was a scattering of straw and a few miniature figurine pieces of Jesus, Mary and Joseph, a few sheep and some cattle. I don't remember saying many, if any, formal prayers in front of that crib or even thinking very deeply about Jesus' impending birth. But in time I've realised watching my own kids do the same, that just placing those pieces in the scene is a prayer in itself.

Apart from loving Christmas, I loved to clean. I remember when I was about seven I would vacuum the house before leaving for school. I have no idea what was wrong with me but it was something that just came naturally. I loved polishing my mother's dressing table and decorating it with her crystal necklace, bracelet and matching clip-on earrings. But most vividly I remember dusting the laminated images of The Sacred Heart of Jesus and The Immaculate Heart of Mary that stood on either side of her dressing table. We also had a medium-sized statue of the Sacred Heart of Jesus standing in the vestibule next to the front door. I loved looking at that statue as it gave me a warm feeling and a certain sense of security. Sometimes I paid little attention as I entered the house and ran past without too much thought. But I know now that even if I was not looking at Him, He was looking at me.

Despite those religious images planting spiritual seeds, they took a while to grow. My First Holy Communion day approached. My grandmother owned a clothing factory and made my communion dress and my mother bought me a most beautiful white veil with lace trim. I felt so special and so beautiful that day as I approached the altar rails to receive Our Lord for the first time. My school was only a couple of blocks from the church and they provided a special breakfast for all the First Communicants. Puffs of white tulle, satin and lace flanked by boys dressed in crisp white shirts, pale blue ties and matching blue sashes bounced elatedly down the footpath as we headed toward the celebratory meal. As I walked along I felt an indescribable joy deep within me. I was momentarily lost in a kind of ecstasy, but suddenly awoken from that childhood rapture by a friend beckoning, "Anne, come on let's run to the breakfast".

This was a very special day in my life. A kiss on my forehead from Jesus at those altar rails. My faith meant a lot to me as I was growing up. My parents had problems and I relied on my faith and daily Mass to get me through. Sadly, with all the upheaval in the Catholic Church after the Second Vatican Council, many people did away with the old traditions and those beautiful statues and icons even disappeared from my family home.

The upheaval seemed to affect everyone in the church. I remember sitting in a boring school assembly with about 1500 students. A nun stepped up to speak. She was talking about friendship and started to describe a student who didn't have any friends. I felt so sorry for this girl and wondered who it could possibly be. I also wondered how they knew she had no friends. Looking toward the stage at the front of the auditorium the nun stooping over the microphone soon answered my question. She informed 1500 students sitting in the auditorium that day that the girl who had no friends attends daily Mass. The girl sitting next to me leant over and whispered, "She's talking about you, isn't she!" Daily Mass was my rock, something I treasured, and now this nun had put a major barrier between me and attending that most precious event. Why would she do that?

My husband and I decided we would teach our children prayers and nurture their religious faith. We took them to Mass on Sundays and during the week. This was not always easy especially in the school holidays when everyone was home. One weekday I loaded the kids into the van and drove down to the nearby church. I breathed in deeply and promised we would go to McDonalds after Mass if they behaved.

Against all odds the little ones were relatively quiet and well-behaved matching the pictures in their Mass books with what the priest was doing. All was good until I left them in the 'crying room' while I went down the front to receive Holy Communion. I always tried to join the end of the communion line so I wouldn't be away from the kids for too long. But on this day, it all unraveled very quickly. After communion I started walking back toward the 'crying room' encouraging my toddler to walk in the same direction as me while trying to balance a baby over my shoulder. Suddenly the prayerful silence of the church was pierced with a high-pitched cry:

"SHIIIIT!!"

Did I hear that correctly? Could one of my kids have yelled that out? Surely they didn't learn that from me!? My face turned into a tomato as I did the walk of shame trying to think how it could possibly be interpreted as a word of prayerful praise. Unfortunately, no, there was no way out of this humiliation. I couldn't even shift blame onto another family, as we were the only ones in the 'crying room' that morning!

But as time went by I dropped the shame and started to care less and less about what people thought. It was empowering.

One morning I only had four of the children at Mass with me the youngest being in a baby capsule. I thought I'd try to sit in the main section of the church and see how we go. Mass started and the children were attentive following their books and the baby was contented. At the consecration I turned to the children to encourage them to look toward the altar and tell Jesus they loved Him. They bowed their heads piously. I felt proud. What good little children. The morning was going well. Feeling I had it all under control I slowly turned my head to the left and noticed that my three-year-old son was in the church aisle and had pulled down his pants! I nearly died. I silently gasped and discretely dragged him by the arm toward me, pulled up his pants and resumed praying as if nothing had happened.

Years later that self-defrocked boy was an altar server frocked in alb and being taught by his older brother how to serve Mass. But too soon they outgrow that stage and don't want to serve anymore. Our parish priest was lucky there was a steady supply of boys from our family. One

Sunday when the boys were much older, we were late for Mass and when we hurriedly found our pew (not easy for our family to find that kind of space), I looked up and noticed there were no altar servers. I quietly asked our boys to serve. They refused. I could see they didn't want to walk onto the sanctuary late in front of everyone. When Father finished the opening prayer, he asked if the altar boys in the congregation could help him serve. He was looking directly at our family. Our boys did not move. Awkward. I elbowed them. They still did not move. Father was eyeballing them and they still didn't respond! Then with a firm look on his face he left the sanctuary and headed toward our pew. I nudged them again and whispered, "He's coming to get you. You better go!" Finally, they gave in and shuffled off.

Years later at another parish, we were celebrating Anzac Day – where Australia and New Zealand commemorate their fallen war heroes. About twelve of us sat in a pew halfway down the middle of the church on the left. I asked the older children to sit next to a younger sibling to ensure they behaved and help them follow the Mass. The priest at this parish was very community minded and would interact with the congregation especially during his homilies. On this day he was walking around handing the microphone around, asking people to say what ANZAC Day meant to them. Old men were making comments about the war and patriotism, others offered prayers for the dead. We usually stayed quiet at those occasions – we weren't used to spontaneous vocal intercessory prayers, or so I thought...

He began to walk back to the sanctuary when he was distracted by a very small raised hand at the end of our pew. One by one like dominoes our heads turned toward the end of the pew. All the way down the end, one of my young boys had his hand up, and next to him, an older boy with a very, very smug smile on his face. I felt sick. What had he put him up to? This could ruin us. There was nothing I could do.

I lowered my head, waiting for the guillotine to drop, thinking of all the crazy, offensive things that might be brewing. The very amused priest handed the microphone over to the six-year-old, who boomed into it saying…

"Australia is the best!"

I breathed a massive sigh of relief as the rest of the congregation laughed. I knew what that older son was capable of, and I remain grateful to the Lord that he chose his words wisely.

Like most Catholic families, devotions in the home are far less pious and far more rowdy than in church. Praying the Rosary together has been the glue holding our family together over the years – I'm convinced of it. But the problem was that my kids were not angelic cherubs. We prayed through teasing and baiting, climbing over lounges, strangling with Rosary beads, somersaults and very out of tune singing. Sometimes I was amused, other times exhausted, wondering what God thought about this craziness.

At the end of the Rosary we would pray the beautiful Litany of Loreto – a collection of titles to Mary the Mother of God. Each night we asked one of the children to lead the Rosary. This meant chosing different siblings to say a decade and then recite the Litany. Our eldest daughter would always chose the brother who had difficulty pronouncing the titles. "Our Lady help of Christians" would become "Our Lady help of Christmas". Because of the ensuing laughter the Rosary would often extend beyond the allocated 20 minutes.

The Rosary brought us together even if we were physically apart, in some very special ways. On one of those camping trips John did with the older kids, they miscalculated the track and some wet weather slowed them down, so they decided to backtrack and had to ask a family on a farm if they could use their barn as a shelter. They were exhausted. One of my sons used their phone to call me, which was providential, as John's 88-year-old father had been taken to hospital with pneumonia. I just told them to pray and I would be in touch.

They were huddled in their barn praying the Rosary, and I was praying at home with the younger kids. During the third mystery my phone rang again. It was my sister-in-law saying my father-in-law had died.

Amazingly she told me they were around his bedside in the hospital in the middle of the third mystery. I hung up and then dialed the farmhouse to get through to John. A gentleman answered. I asked to speak with my husband. He told me it was a bit of a trek down to the barn and it was getting late, so could I ring back tomorrow? I told him my husband's father had just died. He was very compassionate and made the trek immediately down to the barn. I waited nervously on the other end of the phone searching for the right words to use. I heard John pick up the phone, "Hello, is everything alright?"

"John, I have something to tell you, your father's pneumonia worsened. He has just died".

There was stunned silence. I still wonder to this day if I chose the right words. He went on to say they were all praying the Rosary and were on their third mystery.

Traditions are so important to me. As crazy as the Rosary was, it was worth the effort.

And the other one was Christmas.

I just love Christmas with all the decorations, festivities and preparations. One year I bought a traditional Fontanini nativity scene from Rome, so I didn't have to keep making my own every year with cotton wool clouds and an aluminium foil sky. It became the centre of our home, and the young children would play with the figurines just like I used to. John and the kids would set it up with a rust-coloured sheet covering a structure of books and small boxes, then decorate it with bark, sticks and rocks they collected from the garden to form a shelter.

One year I bought a statue of Baby Jesus and placed Him in a small wooden cradle and covered Him with a silk blanket adorned with golden tassels hanging from each corner. The children and now the grandchildren love to tuck Him in each night and kiss his little head after we pray the Rosary in front of the warm glow of the burning Advent candles.

When each child was born I made them a huge Christmas stocking – big enough for them to sleep in! The problem with that is that they were expensive to fill every Christmas... They had different colours and Christmas themes, but mostly green and red and a different coloured trim at the top. I had to fill them with everyday items such as deodorants, underwear, small breakfast cereal boxes, gold chocolate coins, a toy and a book or two. One of my friends taught me that presenting a gift was as important as the gift itself, so we developed the habit of wrapping gifts with ribbons, bows, minature bells, and tasteful wrapping paper. Christmas Day ended with a room full of paper and more or less happy children!

As the years went by the kids grew and so did their senses of humour – well at least for some. One Christmas one of the older boys intentionally mixed up the presents, so we had boys opening boxes of dolls and girls unwrapping footballs. Another year, our youngest son received a huge box wrapped decoratively in Christmas paper and ribbon from a couple of his older brothers. He was so excited and we were intrigued with this amazing and thoughtful present. He ripped off layer after layer after layer of paper revealing more and more boxes. His eyes grew larger and larger in anticipation of what this mysterious gift could possibly be. With every box he opened there was another box, then another and another until he threw away the last piece of wrapping revealing a rather small box. Slowly he opened it only to discover it was empty. He ran off crying – this was definitely hitting below the belt.

One year we decided to introduce a new tradition – the 'Joke Present'. It was a simple gift to take the mickey out of each person based on something incredible, embarrassing or crazy they had done during the year. Of course, mum and dad needed to censor the jokes beforehand as they had a tendency to cause offence, and even the censors couldn't prevent the tears on some occasions… but at least people learnt to have thick skin.

When the children were young we bought a real tree and the boys would help John put it in the bucket and fix it in place, and one child would have the honour of placing the star or an angel on the top of the tree. As time went on they became expensive so we decided to settle for an artifical American-type tree. It looked rather real to me but I think most of the kids liked the real ones better and missed the smell of pine. So when we moved to the U.S. we went to get our own – meandering through the maze of Blue Green Spruce, Frazer Fir, Vermont White Spruce in our beanies, parkas and boots. The soft falling snow stuck to the branches like so many fake ones we had seen before – but it was all real! We kicked small piles of snow as we walked along listening to traditional Christmas Carols sung by Bing Crosby and Michael Bublé.

As our family grew and changed so did our traditions and customs. Our baubles became personalised with our children, children-in-law and grand children's names and hung alongside baubles collected from various places we have travelled to as a family.

I would spend weeks preparing for Christmas, and apart from the stockings and the decorations, I cook. Everything. The turkey. The ham. The roast. Hot potatoes in the oven. Fresh baked bread, and then the desserts. Over the years I would delegate the desserts to the kids, and even though a few had left home, competition was still the way to motivate them so we had a gingerbread house competition, while others made the White Christmas. And I would make the traditional Christmas Cake and pudding with fruit and nuts. The Christmas Cake always seemed to last forever, long after the wrapping paper was cleaned up, decorations taken down, and the dead and brittle Christmas tree taken to the tip.

Christmas has become a time of thanksgiving for all the wonderful people in our lives and all the wonderful opportunities we have been blessed to experience. From the heat of the Australian summer and kids playing in the pool well into the night, to the fairytale of being trapped at home with a huge dump of snow and curling up in front of the fire for a White Christmas, there's really nothing more to dream of.

Most of those happy kids that were running through my doll's house have grown up and left. And now they've got their own doll's houses with their own kids running around. Each new one is gorgeous and I treasure the moments I have with them.

We recently celebrated our 42nd wedding anniversary, and sometimes I thought God was treating us like the chosen people – wandering for 40 years in the wilderness!

But home is where the heart is and my heart is in Australia with most of my children. I moved on from dolls' houses a while back and now I'm looking forward to my real home in Heaven, where I've been assured there are many rooms!

I just hope that at the very least, I get a canopy bed.

Anne Perrottet is a wife and mother with more than 40 years of experience raising and educating her thirteen children in Australia and the United States of America.

She has degrees in Education, Psychology, Community Welfare and Counselling and is currently completing a Masters in Applied Positive Psychology and runs her own private counselling practice.

She is a highly regarded and entertaining speaker, commentator, and writer in which she shares her keen insights and positive approach to family life, education and raising children in today's challenging environment.